Colin Terry is a Lecturer in Science Education at University College of North Wales, Bangor.

# Using Micro-Computers in Schools

Edited by
COLIN TERRY

CROOM HELM
London & Canberra

NICHOLS PUBLISHING COMPANY
New York

© 1984 C. Terry
Croom Helm Ltd, Provident House, Burrell Row,
Beckenham, Kent BR3 1AT
Croom Helm Australia, PO Box 391, Manuka,
ACT 2603, Australia

British Library Cataloguing in Publication Data
Using microcomputers in school.
    1. Computer-assisted instruction − Great Britain
    2. Microcomputers − Great Britain
    I. Terry, Colin
    371.3'9445'0941        LB1028.5
    ISBN 0-7099-2443-7

First published in the United States of America 1984
by Nichols Publishing Company, Post Office Box 96, New York,
NY 10024

Library of Congress Cataloguing in Publication Data
Main entry under title:
Using microcomputers in school.
    1. Education−−Data processing−−Addresses, essays,
lectures. 2. Microcomputers−−Addresses, essays, lec-
tures. I. Terry, Colin.
LB1028.43.U8  1984     370'.28'5      83-8305
ISBN 0-89397-172-3

Printed and bound in Great Britain

# CONTENTS

# Contents

## ACKNOWLEDGEMENTS

The articles appearing in this book are written by some of the leading authorities on the use of microcomputers in schools, both in the U.K. and the U.S.A. I wish to thank each contributor for the submission of their article. The book was compiled during the tenure of a Visiting Scholarship at the University of California, Berkeley. The editor acknowledges the support of the School of Education and the Lawrence Hall of Science at Berkeley during this period. Sincere thanks are expressed also to Catrin Stevens and Carys Thomas for their cooperation, patience and skill in the preparation of the typescript. We hope that this collection of articles will provide a useful reference for all those involved with the education of children and who wish to increase their awareness concerning the role of the microcomputer in the educational process.

Colin Terry
Bangor

# PREFACE

There can be little doubt that educationists, a term that includes teachers, administrators, advisors and inspectors, have caught the fever of interest in Information Technology during the last two years. For some it is a disease which has to be eliminated or it may distract from the traditional well-tried pathway of the system. Others find it so exciting as a subject that they wish to put it in a test-tube and experiment with it, ignoring the widespread effects on the rest of the curriculum. For another group, increasingly the majority, the excitement, enthusiasm and opportunities on offer throughout the school curriculum have encouraged a broader interest in its applicability into every subject area. However, such interest is tempered by lack of knowledge and also a certain anxiety which stems from the enormity of the possible upheaval to the traditional teachers' role. A book like this helps immeasurably to provide information and experiences which add essential knowledge to the teacher's armoury and helps to dispel unfounded suspicion.

To find the source of a teacher's interest in the subject is more difficult as time goes by. Some took up the microcomputer as hobbyists and have become addicted as a result while others have absorbed the numerous stories in the media. Undoubtedly the publicity and activities of the Microelectronics Education Programme (MEP) sponsored by the DES and the Micros in Schools Scheme sponsored by the Department of Industry have helped to encourage this interest as well. The principle concerns of MEP have been in promoting a constantly updated INSET programme, supplying a steady stream of information and contacts throughout its regions and promoting the development and production of teaching and learning materials, devices and software. MEP has acted as a stimulant for activity under national and regional direction, working co-operative schemes with industry, commerce, government, education authorities and above all teachers.

Several of the ambitions and activities of MEP are reflected and illustrated in many of the pages of this book, for there are articles on each of its domains and by many of the people who work for it. Unlike the approach of many other countries, that of the United Kingdom has been notably comprehensive, ranging from the important learning opportunities presented by electronics and control technology to the challenge to the basic approach to learning emerging from information studies and the appearance of major databases. The emphasis is that the impact is not on one or two subjects but right across the curriculum and for all ages of children. Nor are the activities concentrated only on the brightest pupils; the technology provides considerable opportunities for those children with special needs and learning difficulties.

While new materials appear from various units and development agencies, the in-service training of teachers is of great importance in order to ensure that the resources are effectively used in our schools. Such training must be based on an understanding of the range and breadth of the impact of the technology, and it is to the development of this knowledge that this publication makes its contribution. From this background, teachers will hopefully gain an enthusiasm for the benefits of the technology and a creative approach to the redrawing of the curriculum for the future.

Richard Fothergill
Director, Microelectronics Education Programme

## LIST OF CONTRIBUTORS

Harold Abelson is Associate Professor of Electrical Engineering and Computer Science and heads the Educational Computing Group at the Massachussetts Institute of Technology, U.S.A. He worked with Seymour Papert on the development of LOGO and is the author of *Turtle Geometry* (1981) and *Apple Logo* (1982).
Harold Abelson's article is condensed from "A Beginner's Guide to Logo" which appeared in the August, 1982 issue of BYTE magazine. Copyright 1982 Byte Publications, Inc. Used with the permission of Byte Publications, Inc.

Colin Baker is a lecturer in Research Methods in Education at the University College of North Wales. His interests include curriculum evaluation, the use of computers in education and bilingualism.

Graham Bevis is the MEP National Coordinator responsible for microelectronics and technology. He is the Chief Examiner and Moderator of various 'O' and 'A' level courses in electronics. From 1978–1982 he was the Director of the Electronic Systems 'A' level project based at the University of Sussex.

Alfred Bork is Professor of Physics and Director of the Educational Technology Centre at the University of California, Irvine, whose goal is to enhance the learning process through the use of computers. His main interest is in the application of computers to the teaching of concepts in physics. He is a leading international authority on the use of computers in teaching and learning.
The article by Alfred Bork is reprinted from the Proceedings of the University of Oregon's Third Annual College of Education Summer Conference entitled "The Computer: Extension of the Human Mind" Eugene, Oregon, U.S.A. July 1982 by permission of the publisher, the ERIC clearing house on Educational Management, University of Oregon.

Daniel Chandler began teaching English in comprehensive schools in 1974. He is the author of the Study Text for the MEP Micro-Primer scheme and has edited a recent CET publication *Exploring English With Microcomputers*. He is the author of a forthcoming title *Young Learners and the Microcomputer*.

Bill Finzer is a lecturer in Mathematics at San Francisco State University and a consultant with the Software Concepts Group of the Palo Alto Research Centre of the Xerox Corporation. His recent work has included developing curriculum for training teachers to use computers in the teaching of mathematics and developing computer based courseware for schools.

Rosemary Fraser is the Director of the ITMA (Investigations on Teaching with Microcomputers as an Aid) project based at the College of St. Mark and St. John in Plymouth and the Shell Centre for Mathematical Education at the University of Nottingham. Her interests are in the use of the microcomputer as a teaching aid and she is the author of many articles in this field.

Stephen Marcus is an Associate Director of the California South Coast Writing Project. His responsibilities include program design and evaluation and in-service training in computer literacy for teachers of English. He has published extensively on computer-assisted learning and is a member of the editorial board of *Computers, Reading and Language Arts*.

Diane Resek is an Associate Professor of Mathematics at San Francisco State University, where she founded the Centre for Mathematical Literacy. She is currently involved in developing curricula which integrate the use of computers with the teaching of mathematics.
Diane Resek and Bill Finzer wish to acknowledge the Mina Shaughnessy Scholars' Program of the Fund for the Improvement of Post-Secondary Education for support in the preparation of "Computers, Languages and Learning".

Gareth Roberts is Head of Modern Languages, Ysgol David Hughes, Gwynedd. His interests are in the use of microcomputers in the teaching of second languages. He has published several articles in this field and is the author of a forthcoming title on the computer as a resource in the teaching of modern languages.

Nick Rushby is the Director of CEDAR (Computers in Education As a Resource) based at Imperial College, London. His main interests are in computer based learning and in particular its effective use by classroom teachers. He is also responsible for providing support for computer based training for industry. He is the author and editor of a number of books on computer based learning, including *An Introduction to Educational Computing* published by Croom Helm in 1979.

Colin Terry is a lecturer in Science Education at the University College of North Wales. His main interests are in the development of scientific process skills and concepts and the use of computer based learning schemes in schools.

David Trowbridge is the project manager of a computer based program to develop learning skills in early adolescence at the Educational Technology Centre, University of California, Irvine. The materials developed by the project emphasise formal reasoning skills in the context of middle school science and mathematics curricula.
The article by David Trowbridge and Alfred Bork first appeared in Lewis, R. and Jagg, E.D. (Eds.) *Computers in Education*, **325** (1981) published by North Holland Publishing Company. Reprinted with permission.

Peter Weston is a Principal Lecturer at the North East Wales Institute of Higher Education and the Schools Liaison Officer for Computer Education in Clwyd. He is the author of a number of publications on the use of computers in education and is currently directing a school project on word, text and information processing.

# INTRODUCTION

Colin Terry

## The Microcomputer

The computer is not a new innovation. Computers have been used for many years in a variety of applications. The name by which we refer to them is largely due to the fact that they were initially machines devised to perform extensive 'computations' - that is, mathematical manipulations, with great speed and accuracy. But computers can do more than perform high speed calculations. They can be programmed to draw pictures, compose music or stimulate situations that might be too expensive or dangerous to experience in real life. They can store and process large amounts of information easily and quickly or function as a personal tutor in almost any subject area of the school curriculum. One must be careful however not to endow some innate intelligence to a computer. A computer must be told *exactly* what to do, down to the most elementary level and minute detail. The value of the computer lies in the rate at which these commands can be executed.

The uses mentioned so far for the computer are not new, yet only recently have we heard the proclamation that the computer revolution is upon us. Indeed only quite recently have computers made any sizeable impact on our daily lives. This impact is becoming increasingly noticeable and has come about because of significant developments in silicon 'chip' technology. This new microelectronic technology has made possible the construction of sophisticated electronic components that are very much cheaper, very much smaller and very much more reliable than before.

A computer (or perhaps more accurately, a computer 'system') consists of four main components, an input device, an output device, a memory and a central processing unit. The input device, for example a keyboard, allows the user to communicate with the computer. The output device (a television screen or printer) allows the computer to communicate with the user. Information communicated to the computer is stored in the memory. The 'brain' of the system is the central processing unit or CPU, which controls what the computer does. It contains the electronic circuits that

**1**

interpret and execute (or 'process') instructions communicated by the user and directs the interaction of the memory and the input and output devices. This interaction is depicted in **figure I**.

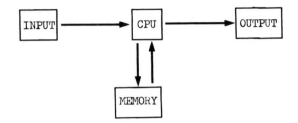

**Figure I: A microcomputer system**

The major technological breakthrough which has been heralded as the 'computer revolution', is the development of the **micro**processor in which all the processing functions described above are built into a single silicon chip. Significantly, microprocessors are cheap to build and buy, small in size and reliable in operation and it is their widespread availability that has led to the microcomputer revolution. A **micro**computer is simply a computer system whose central processing unit is a microprocessor. Computer installations which previously were expensive and occupied a large amount of space were suddenly available at relatively low cost and very much smaller in size. This marked the advent of the 'personal' computer. Consequently it became feasible to consider using computers in a wide variety of situations and applications where previously cost and size would have prohibited such considerations. The car, the bank and the supermarket are all being radically altered by the computer. Businesses are being transformed with computer controlled robots on the assembly line and word processors in the office and we are experiencing revolutionary changes in the way information is generated, stored and transmitted. such is the impact of the microcomputer, and it has all taken place in a very short time span.

**Microcomputers in Schools**

It has been predicted that microcomputers will bring about widespread and fundamental changes in schools. The use of computers in schools is however not new. 'Computer studies' has featured in the curriculum of many schools for some considerable time and the microcomputer will no doubt accelerate the adoption of such courses by more children in more schools. However, an increasing number of teachers are experimenting with the use of microcomputers to enhance their teaching in other areas of the school curriculum. It is the relatively low cost, autonomy and flexibility of the microcomputer that has contributed to this increased awareness and classroom use of the computer. There are those who see the computer as the key to realising many hitherto unrealised educational goals such as promoting pupil-directed inquiry, enhancing the development of scientific and mathematical concepts and addressing more efficiently the learning needs of individual children in mixed ability classrooms or those who are unmotivated, bilingual or in need of remedial teaching etc. There are others who remain more sceptical and point out that given the day to day demands of teaching, most teachers do not have the time and/or skill to take advantage of the computer in the teaching of their particular subject. The sceptics also point to the current, often trivial use of the computer in the classroom, for example, in routine rote learning situations and to the lack of readily available programs (software) of sufficiently high quality. There is quite widespread agreement that the state of the art in educational software development leaves much to be desired but there are signs that the situation is changing. More time, effort and money is being devoted to the production of high quality educational software for schools, and increased opportunities are available for software evaluation.

Whatever arguments are presented for or against the use and usefulness of computers in education, the microcomputer has become an available and flexible resource for the *school*, even though it has yet to become an available and flexible resource for most classroom *teachers*. The potential though is clearly there. It can be a personal tutor, or a simulated laboratory experiment in science. It can keep a record of tests and assessments for the entire class and monitor the progress of each pupil in the class. It can teach and indeed be taught. It can be as valuable or as useless as an overhead projector, a video tape recorder or indeed a blackboard in the teaching of a particular subject in the curriculum. It is an add-on device replacing nothing, a tool to be used in an appropriate way at an appropriate time to improve what is already being done with other resources available to the teacher.

One way to evaluate the use of microcomputers in schools is to define as clearly as possible our educational goals and ask ourselves if the computer can play any sizable part in the realisation of these goals for each child in the classroom. The choice to use or not to use, the choice of when and how to use the computer should become and remain the responsibility of the teacher. We must beware in this choice of attempting to computerize all learning experiences. There are many educationally meaningful experiences that can be provided more effectively without the use of the computer, yet there are many special features of microcomputers that can enhance teaching and learning. It is hoped that this book will provide the reader with a sound sense of the possibilities and limitations of the use of microcomputers in schools and thereby contribute to the decision concerning what use (if any) is to be made of the microcomputer in the classroom.

## Computer Literacy

Schools are charged with the task of ensuring that each pupil reaches a minimum standard of literacy in certain 'basic' subjects; the microcomputer revolution has initiated a demand for 'computer literacy' to be added to the list of 'basics'. It is important to make the distinction between 'computer awareness' and 'computer literacy', two terms which have been the centre of considerable discussion and indeed controversy in recent years (1,2,3). 'Computer awareness' usually means becoming aware of the extent to which computers are part of our lives and the society in which we live. It might include a study of the history of computers, how a computer works, what computers do, where they are used, the impact they are likely to have on society and perhaps the moral and ethical questions raised by the increased use of computers in everyday life. Luehrmann (2) suggests we consider the term 'computer literacy' to be derived from a wider use of the term 'literacy', for example, in language or mathematics. Luehrmann emphasises that literacy in a language refers to the ability to read and write, that is *do* something with the language. Similarly, literacy in mathematics means the ability to *do* mathematics - to do essential arithmetic, solve algebraic equations and so on. The implication for schools is that literacy skills such as these are needed for a person to function reasonably successfully in modern society. The term has recently been extended to include computer literacy which implies the ability to *do* computing, not merely to be *aware* of facts about computers and computing. Such computer literacy can only be achieved by hands-on experience and practice at computing. There is a powerful argument that 'computer literacy' should feature as our prime goal in introducing children to computers, in contrast to the many courses currently available in our schools which are mainly concerned with 'computer awareness'. Unfortunately it takes much more equipment to turn out 'computer literate' pupils than most schools currently possess. Luehrmann proposes a minimum equipment plateau for teaching an effective course in computer literacy of eight computers available one hour per day for each class of thirty pupils. This arrangements allows half of the pupils to work in pairs on a machine in a largely self-instructional situation while the other half is receiving classroom instruction. Although such an arrangement adds only a negligible sum to the running cost of most schools, it is still an unusual one to find today. Increased awareness of the importance of computer literacy for today's children at the LEA and public level, together with some further decline in equipment costs and the advent of new, easier to use programming languages will in due course enable schools to move towards achieving computer literacy rather than computer awareness. However, as Luehrmann points out a significant challenge remains:

> "to define learner objectives for a course that will turn out literate doers of computing and then embody these objectives in a practical curriculum intended for wode adoption. Such a curriculum would have a learner goal of mastering wholly new analytic, expressive and problem-solving skills".

Luehrmann sees computing taking its place as a regular school subject for the same reasons that reading, writing and mathematics are there:

> "Each one gives the pupil a distinctive means of thinking about and representing a problem, of writing his or her thoughts down, of studying and criticising the thoughts of others, and of rethinking and revising ideas, whether they are embodied in a paragraph of English, a set of mathematical equations, or a computer program. Pupils need practice and instruction in all such basic modes of expressing and communicating ideas. Mere awareness of these modes is not worth the time it takes from teaching the creative and disciplined use of these fundamental tools".

Such a challenge can only be met through a long term commitment of all associated with the education of children in our schools.

## In-Service Education

In the education system, outside perhaps the area of computer studies, the microcomputer has often been termed a 'solution looking for a problem'. But computers have much to offer in an educational environment - computer literacy is but one of the many facets of education involved. The learning of languages, science, mathematics or music can also benefit from using the computer in a variety of different ways. Teachers in all areas therefore need to learn about how the computer can be used as a learning environment for their particular pupils, for their particular subject discipline. They need themselves to be literate in all the possible uses of computers in education. For this to take place the teacher must have some level of understanding of computer technology and perhaps some understanding and experience of computer programming. Although teachers of science and mathematics are generally more comfortable with these issues, such awareness and experience is limited among the teaching profession at the present time. Of course very few teachers will be directly involved with the development of computer based learning materials but they will find it desirable to understand the processes involved. Over the next few years many teachers will actively participate in such developments while others will wish at least to understand and perhaps modify for their own use, programs developed by others. The majority of teachers do not therefore need to be expert programmers. However, it would prove of considerable benefit for a teacher to have enough programming experience to be able to read programs and interact with those producing programs for their particular needs. If experienced programmers are to produce software for effective use in schools, answers to questions concerning relevance, pedagogy, sequence, level etc. can only come from the classroom teacher.

Microcomputers are becoming widely available in schools even though the number in any one school is still small. Even when available however, microcomputers are not well used in schools. The microcomputer all too often becomes the personal possession of a relatively small number of staff and pupils. We can expect the rate of purchase to accelerate perhaps as much as a result of parental pressure as increased awareness and commitment of LEA's. This will increase the availability of a computer to many other curriculum areas. An immediate task is to provide the necessary vehicle for school staff development in these areas to match this increased availability. The lack of teacher time is the largest obstacle to any effective program of staff development. The problem is compunded in this case by the limited availability of equipment and the relatively longer amount of time needed for training in computer skills compared with other areas of professional development. It is unlikely that traditional models of in-service education will suffice for the task of training in computer skills and alternative models will need to be explored if any significant progress is to be made. Teachers should not have to spend out-of-school time to become computer literate. Many will voluntarily donate much of their own time but LEA's must be encouraged to allow in-service projects to take place during school time, thereby demonstrating to school staff their own commitment to computer education.

If the goal of a computer literate teaching force is to be met, it is suggested than an on-going in-service education course should be offered from within the school. Each school should consider using their own computer 'experts' who would then be available for follow up questions and problems. The majority of the time should be spent on hands-on experience. The initial exposure should be as non-mathematical as possible and consideration should be given to using microcomputer graphics to introduce teachers to computers and programming. This would give teachers almost instant programming success and provide a higher degree of motivation than that typically generated by more traditional introductory programming courses. It is possible to teach all the basic programming concepts through graphics and the teacher will later be able to apply these skills to more conventional programming problems. The training of teachers across all subject areas in the curriculum to use the microcomputer effectively in the teaching of their subjects represents one of the largest problem areas and is essential if microcomputers are to achieve their considerable potential in schools.

## Microcomputer Hardware

For the next few years the use of microcomputers in education will be in the experimental stage. In many ways todays 'first generation' machines are not particularly suited to educational use. The videoscreen cannot display many characters and it is often difficult to display pictures and text at the same time. Some machines do not have lower case and user interaction through the keyboard is primitive and often unsatisfactory. More sophisticated interaction is possible but remains expensive. The popular microcomputers have limited memory and use microprocessors that operate at only about one tenth as fast as today's designs. We need therefore much more adventurous experimentation in the industry with graphics, colour, videodisc and interaction modes.

However, the present generation of microcomputers will be around for a significant time to come. There is a vast amount of software available for today's machines and for educational use we can expect to see the development of higher quality software. The more software there is available for a machine, the more compelling the reason to buy that particular model, despite other inadequacies it may have. The greater the number of machines there are in use, the greater the incentive to produce software for that machine. We are likely to see then, a continuation of the 'software-driven' market for some time. The major expected change in today's microcomputers is therefore not so much in fundamental design, features or even price but in manufacturing approach with the use of smaller numbers of more sophisticated electronic components inside the computer. Whilst for industrial and business use the demand for larger and faster machines will grow, within education, such demands will not be made if they are in any way at the expense of software availability.

There are still not many microcomputers in schools and the process of introduction will take a relatively long time. Decisions concerning purchase should not therefore involve a consideration of tomorrow's more sophisticated machines, but centre on the details of one's own particular needs and how these needs can be met by currently available microcomputers. Anyone investigating the potential of microcmputers should ask questions such as - what hardware configuration is need to support the quality software available today and in the near future? What memory capacity is required for such programs? How valuable will it be to 'network' several computers in classrooms? What is the importance of high resolution graphics for teaching particular subjects? What programming language capabilities are required? Only with answers to questions such as these will the most effective investment be made.

## REFERENCES

1.    Johnson, D.C., Anderson, R.E., Hansen, T.P., and Klassen, D.L., Computer literacy - What is it?. *Mathematics Teacher, 73,* 91-6 (1980).

2.    Luehrmann, A., Computer literacy - What Should It be?, *Mathematics Teacher, 74,* 682-6 (1981).

3.    Anderson, R.E., Klassen, D.L., and Johnson, D.C., In Defense of a Comprehensive View of Computer Literacy - A Reply to Luehrmann, *Mathematics Teacher, 74,* 687-90 (1981).

# THE FOURTH REVOLUTION - COMPUTERS AND LEARNING

Alfred Bork

"Of all human inventions since the beginning of mankind, the microprocessor is unique. It is destined to play a part in all areas of life, without exception - to increase our capacities, to facilitate or eliminate tasks, to replace physical effort, to increase the possibilities and areas of mental effort, to turn every human being into a creator, whose every idea can be applied, dissected, put together again, transmitted, changed." (I).

The theme of this paper is that we are on the verge of a major change in the way people learn. This change, driven by the personal computer, will affect all levels of education from earliest childhood through adult education. It will affect both education and training. It will be one of the few major historical changes in the way people learn. The impact of the computer in education will not produce an incremental change, a minor aberration on the current ways of learning, but will lead to entirely different learning systems.

This massive change in education will occur over the next twenty years. Schools will be very different at the end of that period. There will be fewer teachers, and the role of the teacher will be different from the role of teacher in our current educational delivery system. I use "schools" throughout this paper in the general sense to include any formal schooling activity, whether it be the primary school or the university, or any other level of education; for emphasis particular types of schools will be mentioned.

I hasten to say that this change will not necessarily be a desirable change. Any powerful technology carries within in it the seeds of good and evil, and that applies to an educational technology. One of the major goals in making presentations of this kind is to nudge us toward a more desirable educational future rather than a *less* desirable one. Our efforts in the next few years are particularly critical for education.

The full, long-range implications of the computer in our world of learning are seldom discussed. Indeed, people are often overwhelmed by the technology, delighted with each new toy which they receive. Yet these implications must be considered if we are to move toward an improvement in our entire educational system. The strategy of this paper will be to first look at the "why," then to look at the "how," and then to return to present action. Many of the issues are discussed in more detail elsewhere (2).

*Why will the Computer become the dominant Educational Delivery System?*

In making a brief case as to why the change I am suggesting will take place, I first look briefly at educational factors in modern society. Then I will consider aspects directly related to the computer.

*Current Status of Education*

First, it does not take any great effort to see that our educational system is currently in trouble. We are being told this constantly from all sides. The daily newspapers, the popular magazines, and recent books are full of descriptions of the problems of our current educational systems. Perhaps the most interesting and critical information is the decline in faith in education in the United States. We can see this very heavily reflected among politicians at all levels. At one time for a politician to speak out against education was suicidal. Now we find that it is often politically effective. Indeed, our current president campaigned on the notion that we had no need for a Department of Education. The entire science education division within the National Science Foundation has been abolished simply by cutting its budget effectively to zero. The politicians know that education has little support in American society and that, indeed, it is politically expedient to cut educational funds. Education has few defenders and many detractors.

I do not wish to imply that these problems with education are simply a matter of public relations. Indeed education has very real problems in this country and elsewhere. In the whole history of the American educational system there has seldom been a time when there was greater turmoil and where the status of teaching, in both the schools and universities, has been lower than it is now. All indications point to the fact that this decline in popular support of our educational system will continue. Few positive factors other than interest in the computer can be pointed to.

Coupled with this declining appreciation of education, perhaps even a consequence, is a factor which affects education even more directly, the factor of increasing financial constraints. The schools do not raise enough money to run an adequate educational system in this country today. Any adequate science or mathematics teacher can earn far more money outside of the schools and universities than that individual can earn within the schools. A few teachers will be dedicated enough to stay with the schools or go to schools in spite of this. But many competent people will *not,* and many people who are not competent to do anything else will teach. These are harsh statements, ones that are not pleasant to hear, but I think they must be made.

Financial constraints manifest themselves in other important ways in education beside teacher salaries. We have had no new major curriculum development at any level in the United States for over ten years. I am referring to sizable curriculum development projects, the type which could lead to improvement in our educational system. Indeed, since the development of the MACOS (Man -A Course of Study) course in the early 1970's, federal funding in curriculum development stopped almost entirely. Ironically, we were just becoming skillful in such development when the funds vanished. What we learned is now being used in large-scale curriculum development in *other* countries.

Another dismal factor in American education is the current classroom environment. Even young children frequently show little interest in education, reflecting widespread parental attitudes. High school classes often seem more like battle fields than educational institutions. This is in stark contrast to what one finds in many other countries at the present time. Hence, American education, and to a lesser extent education everywhere, is in trouble at the moment. It *needs* new approaches and new ways of doing things. Much of the pressure on education is from the outside, and this is the type of pressure which can lead to real change.

> "The teaching profession is caught in a vicious cycle, spiraling downward. Rewards are few, morale is low, the best teachers are bailing out and the supply of good recruits is drying up" **(3)**.

## Computers

When we move from this dismal picture of what is happening in education today to look at the computer situation, the picture is entirely different. The computer, the dominant technology of our age and still rapidly developing, shows great promise as a learning mode. It has been said that the computer is a gift of fire with all the attendant advantages and problems. First, a few hardware comments. Personal computers will be dominant in education. But it is a mistake to believe that computers currently around are the ones I am talking about. We are only at the beginning stage of computer development, particularly with regard to the personal computer. Today's Apples and even today's IBM Personal Computers, considerably more sophisticated than the Apple, are hardly a shadow of the types of machines that will dominate learning. Central processing units are becoming cheaper and more sophisticated, and memory of all types is rapidly dropping in price.

The integrated circuit technology is only at its beginning, and we can expect a long steady decline in prices, increase in capabilities, and decrease in size. Going along with this will be increased educational capabilities, such as sound (both in and out), improved graphics, alternate media, such as those provided by the videodisc, and a host of other rapid developments. In planning for computers in education we must give full attention to this dynamic situation rather than focussing on today's hardware.

Technology is not learning. We can be too carried away with the technology and become interested in it to the exclusion of learning. Therefore we should not give primary attention in education to the new hardware developments. The real interest in the computer in learning lies not in its decreasing price and increasing capabilities, obvious to all, but rather to its effectiveness as a learning device.

How does one demonstrate this effectiveness? In education the traditional mode of experiment has seldom proved to be satisfactory. Neither the financial resources nor the number of subjects are adequate in most existing educational research. The difficulties arise from the many variables which cannot be controlled, so different from the experimental situations that are typical of the physical sciences. Few large-scale experiments have proceeded with the computer, and these were often flawed. Further, our skills in developing materials have advanced, and many of the studies are based on minimal early material. We can find lists of research projects that supposedly do or don't demonstrate that the computer is good in learning, but I am singularly unimpressed with most of these studies when I examine them closely.

So the use of adequate comparison studies in demonstrating that computers are useful in education is seldom practical. All is not lost, however, in demonstrating effectiveness for users. One important way to do this, very convincing in many situations, is to look at some examples of what is possible and to point out the features of those examples which lead to the computer becoming generally very effective in learning. It is this approach we will follow here. Another approach is through peer evaluation, the examination of materials by pedagogical experts in the area involved.

*Educational Technology Centre Projects*

I will describe in this section three projects in computer based learning from the Educational Technology Centre of the University of California, Irvine. The first used a timesharing system; the others, more recent, were developed directly on personal computers.

The first project is a beginning term of a college based physics course for science-engineering students. The key computer materials are the on-line tests, taken at a computer display. Other computer learning materials are also available. The tests contain a large amount of learning material. As soon as a student is in difficulty, he or she is given aid which is specifically related to the difficulty. Each test in unique. Passing is at the competency level; students either demonstrate that they *know* the material or are asked to study further and then take another varient of the test. In 10 weeks we give about 15,000 individual tests to 400 students. The computer keeps the full class records (4).

The second project is concerned with scientific literacy. It hopes to acquaint students with some fundamental notions about science: What *is* a scientific theory or model? How is such a theory discovered? How do we use it to make predictions? What determines if it is a good theory or a bad theory? The material, currently six two-hour units, is designed for a general audience, with initial testing done extensively in the public library. The materials have also been tested in junior high schools, high schools, community colleges, and universities (5).

The third project aims at helping pupils become formal operational in the Piagetian sense. The primary level is the middle or lower secondary school. The format for these units is similar to that for the science literacy materials (6). A description of one of the units is included at a later stage in this book.

## Computer Advantages

Given a brief view of several activities involving the computer in learning, we can now say *why* the computer is such a powerful learning device. At least two factors are critical in considering the effectiveness of the computer in aiding learning, the interactive nature of computer based learning and the ability to individualize the learning experience to the needs of each learner.

One of the major problems in education, particularly education which must deal with very large numbers of pupils, is the fact that we have lost one of the most valuable components in earlier education, the possibility of having learners who are always playing an active role in the learning process. In a Socratic approach to learning, two or three pupils work closely with the teacher, answering questions and therefore behaving as active learners. The process is highly labour intensive. As we had more and more people to educate it became less and less possible to behave in this way. We cannot afford or produce enough master teachers to base our educational system on the Socratic approach. But we *can* develop good computer based learning material in which the student is always *active*. The computer may enable us to get back to a much more humanistic, a much more friendly, educational system by making all of our learners participants rather than the spectators they frequently are in our present book- and lecture- learning environments.

The second advantage offered by the computer is individualization of the process of learning. Everyone says that pupils are different, that each pupil is unique, that each pupil learns in different ways. But most of our standard learning procedures are very weak in allowing for these individual differences. They typically treat most pupils in the same way. For example, if a pupil in a particular point in a course is lacking some important background information, that pupil is swept along in our traditional approaches to teaching with everyone else in the class. The missing information is hard to acquire under those circumstances. The rational procedure would be to allow the pupil needing special help to stop the major flow of learning at that point and to go back and pick up the background information. But most of our present structures for learning have no adequate provisions for such a possibility. The actual needs vary between what can be learned in a few minutes and what can be learned in a whole course.

With the computer the situation is entirely different. Each pupil can move at a pace best for that pupil. Each pupil will be responding frequently to questions. (We have found in our recent programmes that a pupil responds about every fifteen seconds). So the computer, with curriculum material prepared by highly competent teachers, can determine what the learner understands or does not understand at a given point. Remedial aid can be given where appropriate, simply as part of the flow of the material with no break from the learner's point of view. Indeed, the pupil using well-prepared computer based learning material, does not have the impression that any "special" treatment is taking place, so no psychological stigma is attached to such aid. With the individualization possible with computers, one can hope to achieve the goal of mastery learning, where everyone learns all material essentially perfectly.

So much for "why" computers are going to become the dominant educational delivery system. The two factors mentioned, the unpleasant situation in education today and the usefulness of the computer as a way of learning particularly in dealing with large numbers of pupils, suggest that the computer will move rapidly forward in education. But we still must look at the other side of the question, the "how" of the development. That is, how do we move from our present situation, where computers are little used in learning, to a situation in which they are the dominant delivery system? This is the subject of the next section.

*How will we move to greater Computer use?*

Let me first recapitulate earlier information. The period ahead in education, for at least ten years and probably longer, is likely to be characterised by a series of continuing problems. The traditional methods of preserving the status quo in education, or allowing only small incremental changes to take place, such as the power of the administrators and the unions, will have relatively little effect; much of the turmoil in schools will be imposed from the general community. Often changes will be generated by financial decisions which lead to less money to the schools. The challenge will be the most serious one that has been seen in a very long time in the educational system.

The following comment by Peter Drucker gives a view of the situation from outside academia:

"In the next ten or fifteen years we will almost certainly see strong pressures to make schools responsible for thinking through what kind of learning methods are appropriate for each child. We will almost certainly see tremendous pressure, from parents and pupils alike, for result-focused education and for accountability in meeting objectives set for individual pupils. The continuing professional education of highly educated mid-career adults will become a third tier in addition to undergraduate and professional or graduate work. Above all attention will shift back to schools and education as the central capital investment and infrastructure of a 'knowledge society' " (7).

Thus, we will have a society more and more unhappy with the current educational system, a society groping for new ways to handle education. Few "solutions" to the problem will be apparent.

*Home Computers*

During the same period of time computers, particularly personal computers, will be decreasing in cost, increasing in capabilities, or (more likely) some mixture of these two trends. The changes will often be drastic. While the term one hears in the computer industry, zero cost hardware, is intentionally something of an exaggeration, it does reflect what is happening in many areas of computer technology.

One aspect of the rapid development of personal computers that will be extremely important for the future of education will be the increasing presence of the computer in homes. Homes will represent the largest possible market for personal computers, since in no other situation can one speak of millions of units. There are approximately eighty million American homes; so the number of computers which can be sold for home use, provided the ordinary person can be convinced that the computer is valuable to own, is enormous. The home will be the driving force for education too, since the commercial pressures for home sales will be very great. In a sense, education is never "first" with computers. For many years we piggybacked on essentially a business or scientific technology in computers with education only a poor follower. The new situation will be similar, but with the home market the dominant one.

To sell computers for the home, it will be necessary that they *do* something. The average home owner is not going to buy a computer on the grounds that they are currently being sold to homes, primarily for hobbyists. The home user of equipment buys an *appliance*, a device such as a refrigerator or stove that accomplishes some task or tasks. They do not buy a gadget that they can put together in various ways to accomplish different types of tasks. The size of the home market will depend on the skill of vendors in convincing people that the computer in the home will be *useful* to the average person. Some estimates have suggested sixty million computers in homes in ten years.

I do not wish to imply that a single appliance-like use of the computer will drive the home market. On the contrary, a variety of such uses are likely to be important. Home word processing, for example, will be an extremely important use. Home financial systems, complete enough to keep all the financial records and write the income tax when asked to, and to aid in home financial decisions, will also be of importance. Personal record keeping systems, including class notes, lists, and similar uses, are also likely to be of major use in the home. Finally, educational material will be one of the types of material that without question will drive the home market. The size of this market will depend on the quality and quantity of such appliance-like programs.

Thus, we will find learning material based on the computer being developed for home computers, in some cases almost independently of whether it will also be usable in primary and secondary schools, university, or other learning environments. Schools *will* use the material developed primarily for education in the home even though it may not be ideally suited. It may be that this material will often have more careful thought put into it than some of the earlier products developed particularly for the school environment, simply because the potential market is so much larger and users more discriminating. Schools are already desperately searching for computer based learning material and are finding that little good material is available.

The people who are using the new learning materials in the home will be coming to our schools and universities. They will already have become accustomed to interactive learning, and more and more they will demand it in educational institutions. If the educational institutions wish to survive, they will provide it. This may seem a very market-oriented point of view but we must be realistic in trying to plot the future. We must understand that the most fundamental issues that will determine the future *are* these marketing issues, not the academic issues which may be at the forefront of our own minds.

*Companies*

When we look at the school market, we see interesting commercial pressures. The dominant sellers of educational materials to schools today are the commercial textbook publishers. Yet commercial textbook publishing is a static domain at almost all levels of publishing. That is, it is difficult for a company to make much progress there, in the sense of increasing profits. Education itself is getting declining amounts of money. There will be declining numbers of pupils for several years. The competition between companies is fierce. To end up with a much larger share of that market at the present time, considered purely as a textbook market, is extremely difficult. Therefore it is not surprising that many of the most influential textbook publishers are now beginning to devote sizable amounts of effort, attention, and money to computer based learning. They see this as a new market, where it is not at all clear at present who will become dominant. Thus, a minor textbook publisher could see the possibility of becoming a major computer based learning publisher, or a major publisher could see that computer based materials would very much increase revenues. Or a new company could see this as a particular opportunity for advancement, allowing them to leap over the established companies. All these situations are happening now.

The list of textbook publishers putting sizable resources into computer based learning is a distinguished one. It includes such names as John Wiley, Harper & Row, McGraw-Hill, Longmans and many others. The type of involvement is different in different companies - this is, after all, a new market, one that is poorly understood by everyone. The degree of involvement also differs from company to company and is likely to differ in time.

In addition to these established companies, new companies, often particularly devoted to either educational software or to personal computer software more generally, are coming into existence. Sizable amounts of venture capital are available for such companies. These companies, old and new, will be selling their wares, and so more and more school authorities will be able to easily acquire computer based learning materials. Both old and new companies will have people actively soliciting school business. The older textbook companies may want to tie in the computer material with their existing textbooks, but the newer companies will have no need for this, and so may be open to more adventuresome activities. Some of the companies will be selling to a combination of the home and school market. In general the materials developed for the home market will be available in the school market also.

*Schools*

Given the financial restraints in the schools, the commercial pressures, the pressures created by the home market, and the increasing effectiveness of the computer as a learning device, more and more schools will turn to computers for delivery of learning material. One interesting sign is the fact that there are schools that do not have adequately prepared teachers to teach some of the important courses in the curriculum. Thus if we look at high school courses such as advanced mathematics and science courses, rural schools in the United States presently are often not providing these capabilities, at least not in a way that is competitive with the better large urban schools. Computers will be a mechanism for equalizing opportunity for pupils by providing computer based learning courses in these declining areas, courses that otherwise would not be available. Hopefully, these courses will be developed by the best individuals from all over the country.

We may see a decreased role of the formal school and the formal university in our educational system. Much education will be able to take place in the home in a flexible fashion. At the university level we already see one outstanding example of a development of this kind in The Open University, but still with relatively little use of computers. The Open University has demonstrated that good curriculum material in home environments can be effective as a learning mode and economical when compared with the standard cost of education. Voucher systems, if they are enacted, will make home learning much more likely.

I do not wish to imply that all education will move to the home. Indeed, a view of the educational system such as that shown in George Leonard's book, *Education and Ectasy*, suggests that the sociological components, the factors associated with living with other people and living with oneself, will still probably best take place in small group environments within schools. But many of the knowledge-based components of learning may move to the home.

*Types of Usage*

We have discussed very little about the *way* computers will be used within the school system. Something needs to be said about this, if only to counteract some of the current propaganda. The computer will be used in a *very wide variety* of ways within our educational system. The notion that some "right" way exists to use the computer, and that other modes of computer usage are somehow wrong, is one that has been promulgated by a number of individuals and groups in recent years. Indeed, often staged debates at meetings comparing types of usage have been held, with the implication that there are right and wrong ways to use the computer in education. Books have been organized in such a way that it sounds as though there were a competition for different types of computer usage.

These debates, often on philosophical grounds, have made a tacit assumption that a right way to use the computer exists, if only that way could be discovered. Mostly the authors have had a naive belief in their "right way", and then set out to try to establish a case for their beliefs. The principal problem with this type of reasoning is that it often does not proceed from instructional bases, nor does it proceed from empirical bases or experimental studies. That is, the issues that dominate are often technological issues, the nature of the computer hardware and what can be done with the computer hardware. These writers are trying to carve some unique niche for the computer among other learning media.

These technologically-based and media-based arguments for a single type of computer usage are, I believe, entirely misleading. The decisions as to how to use computers - the modes of computer usage, the areas - should be made entirely on *pedagogical* grounds, the questions of what aids learners rather than on these philosophical, media, or technological grounds. Whenever decisions are made on

**18**

pedagogical grounds, it will be found that a wide variety of computer uses will be employed, uses which are often adapted to the individual situation being considered. There is no single "right" way to use computers, but rather a great variety of ways.

I will give a brief classification of the various ways the computer can be used. This list is not exhaustive nor does it show fine detail. But it may be useful to at least consider the range.

## Computer Literacy

Computer literacy is ill-defined and so much debated. It is recognized that at all levels of education, starting perhaps as early as eight or nine years old and continuing through the school system, university, and adult education, that individuals in our society need to understand the various ways the computer is going to be used in that society; they need to understand the positive and negative consequences of those ways. Few full-scale computer literacy courses exist. Indeed, what often passes as computer literacy is vague history or learning to program in a simplified way, to be discussed in a moment. So this is still very much an open area for computer uses. Specialized courses are needed for each group addressed; thus, computer literacy for teachers is a pressing national issue. All these courses need to consider such important future uses as word processing, personal financial and record keeping systems, and educational material.

## Learning to Program

Learning to program is already a rapidly increasing activity in our universities and schools. It represents in secondary schools the most common usage of computers at the present time. Unfortunately, where it happens at this level it is often a *disaster*, harming more than helping the pupil. The major problem is the way programming is taught. A whole group of people is being taught a set of techniques which are no longer adequate to the programming art today. These techniques were common in the early days of computing, but they are inadequate according to today's standards. Many of the people learning to program in schools cannot overcome the initial bad habits which have often been instilled in them when they come to the universities. Many universities are now reporting this phenomenon.

The main culprit is BASIC. It is not that BASIC has to be taught in a way that is antithetical to everything we know about programming today. But it almost inevitably *is* taught in such a fashion. *BASIC is the junk food of modern programming.* Indeed, the analogy is close in that junk food tends to destroy the body's desire for better types of food. But the analogy is weak in one regard: BASIC is the initial language of the vast majority of these people. It is as if you started feeding junk food to babies one day old and give them nothing else until they were six! If I could leave one message, perhaps the most pressing message, it is to *STOP TEACHING BASIC*. It is becoming clear that students who learn BASIC as their first computer language will in almost all cases acquire a set of bad programming habits. These habits are very difficult to overcome, so BASIC programmers have difficulty writing readable and maintainable code.

The following recent comment by a dinstinguished computer scientist, Edgar Dijkstra, is relevant:

"It is practically impossible to teach good programming to students that have a prior exposure to BASIC; as potential programmers they are mentally mutilated beyond hope of regeneration" (8).

What programming languages should we teach? There are a number of possibilities for both primary and secondary schools. LOGO is certainly one interesting possibility, although I must confess that some features of LOGO are different from those recommended in the best modern programming practices. LOGO, however, is introduced in a problem solving environment, and that is very much to its advantage. Often its main intent is presented not to teach programming but to teach more general problem solving capabilities or some specific area of mathematics. But its general problem solving effectiveness has yet to be demonstrated in our mass school environments with ordinary teachers.

Another possibility is PASCAL or a PASCAL-like language. The material developed at the University of Tennessee and sold by McGraw-Hill under the name of *Computer Power* is an excellent example of an approach of this kind. If one looks for print materials that are usable at the secondary school and perhaps even at a lower level at the present moment, the *Computer Power* material seems to be one of the best possibilities. Another approach is to develop some interesting capability based on a structured programming language. For example, the recent *Karel, The Robot* from Wiley follows such an approach. Turtle geometry, in Logo, is the best known example.

*Learning Within Subject Areas*

Undoubtedly the largest use of the computer in schools at all levels will eventually be not the categories just discusssed but rather the use of the computer as an aid in learning mathematics, in learning to read, in learning to write, in learning calculus, and in all the other tasks associated with the learning process.

One person may work alone at a display or several may work together. When one looks at these learning tasks in detail, again one finds a great variety of computer use, ranging from tutorial material, to intuition building, to testing, to aids in management of the class for the pupil (feedback on what is needed and how to go about getting it), and the teacher. The three projects presented earlier show

something of the range of possibilities.
Unfortunately, much of the material now available of this type is very primitive. We are, however, rapidly learning to develop better material to aid learning.

*Production Process*

If we are to move to meet this new future, where the computer will be the dominant educational delivery system, a critical aspect will be the generation of effective learning material. We need new courses and entire new curricula, spanning the entire educational system. Hence, the development we are talking about is a nontrivial process. It is the degree of success of the development process that will tell whether we will improve or damage education. We must convince the likely distributors that it is important to develop quality materials, not the poor quality resources mostly available today.

The development of curriculum material in any field and with any medium and at any level is a difficult process. It cannot be done by amateurs who are doing it simply as a spare time activity. Many new observers in this field, looking at the problems quickly, tend to underrate these problems of developing effective learning material. Hence, some of the solutions which have been proposed are solutions which are simply not adequate to the problems. Some of these solutions assume only small incremental changes in the curriculum structure and do not understand the magnitude of the development necessary.

Several critical points concerning products should be made to give the reader a reasonable overall viewpoint. The production system is a complex system, one that should involve many types of people with many different skills. If one looks at the production of *any* educational material, one sees that that is the case. We can learn much by examining effective curriculum production systems, such as that currently in use in The Open University, that used in producing the major curriculum efforts in the United States more than ten years ago, and that involved in such areas as the development of textbooks. We need to resist the notion that one person, perhaps a teacher in his or her spare time, will do it all. I do not believe that any sizable amount of good curriculum material will be produced by this method. Furthermore, I do not believe that the devices which are being urged for these teachers, such as simple-minded authoring systems based on toy languages (PILOT) will be effective. Nor do I think that languages such as TUTOR will be effective, because they do not meet the reasonable criteria associated with modern programming languages. Most of these languages are old in their design, and few of them understand the nature of structured programming. A serious professional approach is needed if we are to maintain the quality of the computer based learning materials produced.

We can see a number of stages needed in such a professional

approach, listed below.

(a)  Preplanning
(b)  Establishing goals, objectives, and rough outlines
(c)  Specifying the materials pedagogically
(d)  Reviewing and revising this specification
(e)  Designing the spatial and temporal appearance of the material
(f)  Designing the code
(g)  Coding
(h)  Testing in-house
(i)  Revising
(j)  Field testing
(k)  Revising

The last two stages may be repeated twice.

In the entire process, the educational issues as opposed to the technical issues, should be dominant. The best teachers and instructional designers should be involved in stages (c) and (d) to assure the quality of the product.

*Present Steps*

This paper has presented an overview of some of the problems associated with reforming an entire educational system during the next twenty years. Many details are either not mentioned or treated very hastily. But I hope I have given enough details to convince you of the main directions that need to be taken.

As teachers, we are undoubtedly interested in what we should do now to work towards a more effective future for education. First, we must decide whether we would wish to be involved in the type of curriculum development suggested. If we do wish to be involved, we must take a long-range view of how to prepare for this activity.

I would *not* advise you to purchase one of the popular machines and start to use it! Nor, as you might suspect, would I advise you to take courses in BASIC. But it would be desirable to take a variety of courses, if they are accessible to you or to study on your own, in certain areas. Here are some suggestions. The first three refer to areas of learning, either through formal courses or through informal methods.

1.  *Learning theory.* Good curriculum development cannot be developed without some appreciation of how people learn, even though there is no single coherent theory there. Courses in learning theory may help, based on the research literature concerning learning.

2.  *Curriculum development.* The question of how to develop good curriculum material is one that deserves serious study. Some universities provide such courses. Some textbooks exist. Many of the issues are independent of computers, referring to development with any learning media.

3. *Modern programming languages.* You might wish to become acquainted with modern programming languages, such as PASCAL. Again, you must be careful here. It is possible to meet these languages either in an old fashioned environment or in one that stresses structured programming. You want the second possibility. Look at the textbook. If it does not introduce procedures until a third of the way or even further along, do not take the course. This is not the only factor, but it is a good way of distinguishing reasonable from unreasonable courses.

Avoid the "CAI" languages - they are inadequate, not suitable for serious material. Look at the authorising approaches based on modern structured languages.

4. *Listen to pupils.* In your own teaching, begin to move away from the lecture mode presentation into a more Socratic mode. A critical factor is listening to what pupils say and watching what they do. This means that when you ask questions, you have to *wait* for answers. It also means working more individually with pupils in groups of two to four. It is only by this procedure that you will begin to build up the insights you need for how pupils actually behave when they are learning.

People whose primary mode of interaction with pupils is through the 'presentation' mode or through textbooks are seldom the best choices for preparing computer based learning material. The development of computer based learning material will need vast numbers of experienced teachers, teachers who have been listening to their pupils and who understand pupil learning problems.

5. *Personal computers.* Begin to use a variety of personal computers, with particular emphasis perhaps on the newer machines. Read the journals that tell you about new equipment. Watch for voice input, improved graphics, and full multimedia capabilities.

6. *Critical attitude.* Examine computer based learning material, trying to develop a critical attitude toward it. Do not be overwhelmed simply because it is interactive or because the computer is involved. Keep your mind on the learning issues and learn to develop some sensitivity as to what existing material helps learning and what doesn't.

Most existing material is poor. Find out why. Read the journals that specialize in *critical* reviews.

7. *Work with others.* The development of good computer based learning material is best done in a group. Work with others in discussing goals, strategy, and the details of design.

8. *Future orientation.* Concentrate on the long-range situation, not today or tomorrow. Decisions which are "good" from a short-range point of view may be undesirable in the long range to both you and to the future of our entire education system. So keep the long-range point of view strongly in mind.

9. *Visions.* Begin to think about what type of future educational system would be both desirable and possible. If you want to influence the future, you must have visions.

"Developing quality computer-assisted instruction demands forethought; those of you who are unfortunately caught up in expedient movements in education need to take a closer, more courageous look at the nature of the hope on Pandora's chip. You are dealing with as powerful a tool as the gods have ever given us" (9).

## REFERENCES

1. Shervan-Schreiber, Jean-Jacques, *The World Challenge*. Simon and Schuster from The Mitsubishi Report.
2. Bork, A., *Learning with Computers*, Digital Press, Billerica, Massachusetts, (1981).
3. Boyer, E., quoted in Report on Educational Research (February 3, 1982).
4. Bork, A., Computer-based instruction in physics, *Physics Today*, *34*, 9 (1981).
5. Bork, A., Kurtz, B., Franklin, S., Von Blum, R., Trowbridge, D., Science Literacy in the Public Library, Association of Educational Data Systems, Orlando, (February 1982).
Von Blum. R., Computers in informal learning: A case study (November 1980).
Arons, A., Bork, A., Collea, F., Franklin, S., and Kurtz B., Science literacy in the public library - Batteries and bulbs. Proceedings of the National Educational Computing Conference, Denton, Texas (June 1981).
6. Trowbridge, D. and Bork, A., A computer based dialog for developing the mathematical reasoning of young adolescents, Proceedings of the National Educational Computing Conference, Denton, Texas (June 1981).
7. Drucker, Peter F., *The Changing World of the Executive*, Times Books (1982).
8. Dijkstra, Edgar W., How do we tell truths that might hurt?, *SIGPLAN Notices*, *17*, 5 (1982).
9. Quote from Burns, H., Pandora's chip: Concerns about quality CAI, *Pipeline* (1981).

# STYLES OF COMPUTER BASED LEARNING

Nicholas Rushby

## Pupils and Information

The mileau of educational computing abounds with Lewis Carroll like phrases which authors use to mean just what they want them to mean, nothing more and nothing less. The literature is confused with near synonyms such as computer aided instruction and computer aided learning which are sometimes used interchangably, but for some authors have subtle differences of meaning. Certainly there is a difference between the processes of learning and instruction; instruction is not a necessary condition, and is seldom a sufficient condition, for learning. The difference between computer assisted learning (or CAL) and computer managed learning (or CML) is more significant but difficult to define. Traditionally, the distinction has been that in computer assisted learning the learning material is presented to the learner through the computer, while in computer managed learning the computer is used to direct the learner from one part of the course to another and the learning materials themselves are not kept in the machine. So in CAL the learner receives some detailed tuition from the computer and with CML he and his teacher get information about his performance and progress. However, many CAL systems also carry out some management functions. Similarly, some CML systems present tutorial information which would usually be associated with computer assisted learning. The difference between the two is therefore somewhat blurred.

In a simplistic view of the learning process, the pupil acquires knowledge by receiving information from his surroundings and organising it so that he can then retrieve specific items, make generalisations and extrapolations. The speed, and perhaps the quality, of some learning may be improved if the pupil works with structured learning materials and is given some individual guidance by his teacher on his selection of a route through the modules. This implies that the learner will supply information about his progress, problems and preferences. Hence there is a two way flow of information with facts and guidance coming from the environment to the learner, and feedback coming from the learner. This is illustrated in Figure I.

**25**

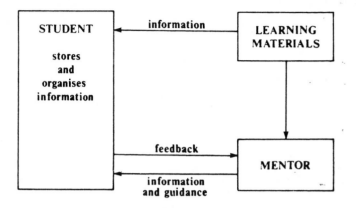

**Figure I: The Learning Environment**

Clearly this is but a crude and oversimplified model of the very complex processes which constitute learning; processes which we do not fully comprehend. It can be argued that until we have developed a better understanding of the learning process it is difficult to advance our use of educational technology. Perhaps, but then there are many teachers who are able to help their pupils to learn although they too lack a clear and complete theory of learning and it seems reasonable that we should proceed cautiously in advance of the theory.

This pragmatic view provides a convenient description of the various types of educational computing. The computer can be seen as a mediator of the two way flow of information between the learner and his learning environment. We have seen that there are various kinds of information, facts, feedback and guidance. There are also quantitative and qualitative differences in the information, depending on the scale at which the learning is examined. At the micro level, for example when the pupil is working in a small group or is reading a book, the information is highly detailed and changes very rapidly. It is difficult to record and store all the information which is passed around during a discussion, yet this is only a small part of each pupil's learning activities during a course which lasts for several weeks, months or years. In the longer term, this level of detail is unnecessary and a summary of the flow is more relevant. So there is another scale at which the learning process can be viewed, where the information is rather less detailed and changes less rapidly. This might be at the level where the pupil's activities are seen in terms of modules which take perhaps two or three hours to complete.

Progressing further, this information can again be summarised to provide details of the learning process on a timescale which spans months, terms or years. Again there is less detail and a slower rate of change of information. This range of information detail and change is shown in Figure 2.

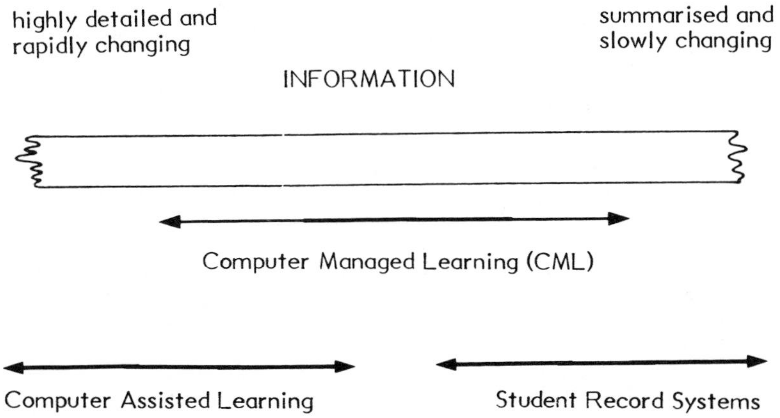

Figure 2: The Spectrum of Educational Information

We should remember that the basic information considered in the model is the same throughout the range; it is the level of detail that is changing. At each stage the information is summarised and so reduced in quantity before being passed onto the next stage. So at the detailed end of the range there is a vast amount of information relating to each of the courses or course fragments which the pupil is using. As the information is summarised, individual fragments are combined to build a more complete picture of his studies. Deliberately, there are no boundaries shown between the separate stages because no real boundaries exist - each stage merges into the next. In considering the learning process, the pupil and his teacher will use an appropriate level of detail which will depend on the individual and the course.

The different applications of computers to the learning process can now be described in terms of the way in which they mediate in the flow of information and of the levels of detail with which they are concerned.

Thus, Computer Assisted Learning (CAL) systems are involved with rapidly changing, highly detailed information and appear at the left side of the range. Computer Managed Learning (CML) systems operate with less detailed information towards the middle of the range. Pupil record systems appear at the right hand side and are concerned only with highly summarised accounts of the pupils' activities and results.

**27**

Lest it should seem that the definition of these terms is unduly belaboured, we should note that the confusion in the terminology of different authors has been the source of many misunderstandings and misconceptions by their readers.

## Justifications

The introduction of computer assisted and computer managed learning in different institutions at different times may be ascribed to a variety of reasons, some of which are altruistic, some more selfish. Three objectives are often advanced in support of the innovation. It is said that CAL will provide:

- savings in costs and resources;
- more effective education or training;
- intellectual challenge.

Firstly, it may be claimed that the new techniques will save time or effort, or both, and hence will either save the institution money, or enable the available staff to teach more pupils. Secondly, other things remaining equal, the same staff with the assistance of the computer can improve the quality of their teaching and their pupils' learning. A third reason is that the innovation will provide an intellectual challenge to the teachers with possibilities for evaluating courses more thoroughly and providing opportunities for a critical appraisal of their pupils' learning. A final incentive, infrequently expressed, is that CAL and CML are stimulating and charismatic; participants in this new area acquire an enhanced professional reputation. While the novelty of most innovations holds considerable appeal, this effect is particularly apparent where computers are concerned. Many people find programming and the mechanics of computing irresistably attractive; some may even get addicted, as if to a drug, and exhibit withdrawal symptoms if they are separated from their computer. This may present a humorous picture, but it does pose a severe problem because the enthusiast's interest in the computer may obscure his judgement of its worth in a particular application. As we will see, there is no good reason why a teacher must learn to write computer programs in order to use CAL. We should beware of forgetting our educational aims in the computing fervour. A detailed understanding of how computers work and how to write computer programs is not a prerequisite for using them effectivley in teaching. In some instances it may help by making the teacher more independent of specialist assistance, but the lack of programming skills or an empathy with computers is not, and should not be, a barrier to using them effectively in teaching. Consider, as an analogy, the overhead projector. In order to use an overhead projector successfully, the teacher must learn some basic rules about making and presenting transparencies, but need not know how to design the complex fresnel lens that is at the heart of the device.

## Educational Paradigms

In the previous section, Computer Assisted Learning (CAL) was described in terms of the kind of information flowing between the learner and his learning environment, mediated by the computer. CAL is characterised by a flow of rapidly changing, very detailed information with the computer playing a prominent role as mediator. However, there are a number of different types of CAL and we must now seek a suitable framework within which to discuss their educational implications. Of the several possible frameworks, that proposed by Kemmis and his colleagues is the most useful in this instance. They invented four educational paradigms which they found to be useful in relating computer assisted learning to the general field of education. The four paradigms are

- the instructional;
- the revelatory;
- the conjectural; and
- the emancipatory.

## The Instructional Paradigm

The early forays into computer assisted learning grew out of the use of programmed learning, particularly in North America. Subsequently, the technique was taken up, albeit on a smaller scale, in Europe and the Soviet Union. Behind the practice of programmed learning, lies a theory of conditioning which owes much to Skinner. This proposed that the best way of learning the subject matter was to break the learning task into many small tasks and then to concentrate upon each of these in turn. The learner would be given a reward to reinforce his learning each time he demonstrated that he had mastered one of these tasks, and would then be allowed to progress to the next. If he encountered problems on a particular task, then he would be held at that point until he had mastered it, or alternatively directed to some remedial work in which the offending task was presented in a different way or possibly broken down into even smaller parts. The key was to divide the subject matter into parts so small that the learner had the best possible chance of learning, and his learning was reinforced at every opportunity. Skinner's original theory has since been modified and embodied as part of other more complex theories, but can still be seen as the basis of much of the present day programmed learning which seeks to rationalise the teaching learning process, sequencing the presentation of material and emphasising feedback to the pupil on his performance. The focus of the instruction is on the subject material and on the pupil's mastery of the various facts and concepts within it.

This approach makes a number of assumptions about the nature of the subject matter; in particular, it assumes that it can be broken up into small parts, each with clearly defined prerequisites and objectives, so that the individual parts can be sensibly structured into

**29**

a coherent sequence, also with clear prerequisites and objectives. That this is possible, is more obvious for some subjects than for others. It also assumes that pupils conform to the behaviourist learning model. Again, it is not obvious that all of them respond to stimuli in the way that the theory assumes.

Clearly, while the theory of programmed learning may be attractive, its implementation poses a number of problems. The breaking of the subject matter into small, well defined learning tasks was then, and is still, a highly skilled manual process, placing great demands on the teaching staff. Once the course has been devised, there are still substantial problems of controlling the pupils' progress through the individual steps, of checking their understanding at each step, and of general management. These latter functions are more easily automated, and it was on them that the early computer assisted learning programs and systems focussed.

## Instructional Dialogue

The association in teachers' minds of programmed learning with CAL has already been lamented, because, as we have seen, CAL is more than just a means of administering programmed texts. Nevertheless, this form of CAL is probably the most widely known and the most readily appreciated. It is relatively easy to make a computer program which can carry out a very restricted dialogue with a pupil on a particular subject. This unit of dialogue, sometimes called a frame, relates closely to the typical programmed instruction (PI) unit. It starts with some text for the pupil to read. In a PI text this would be printed on a page of the book; in the CAL environment it is printed or displayed on the computer terminal. At the end of the text the pupil is asked some questions. It is here that the CA unit starts to demonstrate its greater flexibility. The PI text can pose questions for the pupil but must rely on the pupil's honesty and correct use of the text in checking the answers. In contrast, the CAL program can carry out some limited checking of the pupil's response and give an appropriate reply. At the end of the unit the computer makes a decision based on the built in rules specified by the package designer, as to which unit should be presented next.

So, although in this sample form of CAL the dialogue between the pupil and the computer is very restricted, there are obvious improvements in the feedback to the learner and in the control of his progress over that which can be achieved with a PI text. It is important to remember that the dialogue, the feedback and the rules which govern the sequence in which the subject material is presented are under the control of the designer of the CAL package; the use of CAL is not a valid excuse for the teacher to abdicate his educational responsibilities. As a corollary, we must be careful not to confuse those values associated with the learning process with the values of the learning itself. There are two separate areas that must be examined - the educational values behind the organisation and teaching of the subject material and the means of administering that material to the learner. These two areas may be defined as the technology of education and technology in education.

The appeal of this form of CAL, is that, once the educational material has been developed and polished, the computer can act as an individual tutor of unlimited patience (albeit of limited intelligence) to each of a large number of pupils. It is usually seen as a means of reducing the teacher's load in the particular part of the course in which it is used, thus freeing him to devote more effort to those parts which are taught by other means. Hence, while on a small scale it may be viewed as a teacher substitute, when the course is seen as a whole, it is apparent that the CAL component is being used to complement the teacher rather than to replace him.

It was soon clear that the main technological limitation on the instructional form of CAL was the very restricted dialogue available between the learner and the computer. The dialogue was restricted both in its ability to match the learner's alternative responses against those which had been anticipated by the package writer and also in its field of discourse, in that the computer could only recognise pupil responses relating to a small part of the subject currently under discussion. Even when the material was structured by the course designer to take advantage of the computer's ability to direct the pupil along particular paths and so adapt the tutorial to his individual needs, the pupil was still constrained to follow those prespecified paths embodying the teacher's logic. This constraint was addressed by the later development of the conjectural form of CAL.

**Drill and Practice**

Another use of CAL, Drill and Practice, also falls within the instructional paradigm. In a Drill and Practice lesson the pupil is presented with a structured succession of exercise questions designed to give him practice in a particular technique. The questions can be written into the CAL package, can be drawn at random from a collection of suitable questions called an item bank or, in some cases, can be generated within the CAL program. This latter approach may be suitable for numerical questions which can consist of skeletons that are completed by the program when the questions are used. The program can provide reasonable random values for the calculation and then determine the correct result for checking the pupil's response. The sequence of examples can be arranged so as to provide questions of prespecified difficulty, or can be graded in severity to probe the pupil's learning difficulties. The package can then turn to the simple instructional dialogues discussed earlier to provide remedial tuition in those areas of weakness.

**The Revelatory Paradigm**

As its name implies, this form of CAL guides the learner through a process of learning by discovery in which the subject matter and the underlying theory are progressively revealed to him as he proceeds through the CAL package. Whereas in the instructional form the computer is used to present the subject material, to monitor the pupil's responses and to control his progress through the course module, in revelatory CAL the computer acts as a mediator between the learner and a hidden model of some real life situation. As the learner interacts with the model hidden within the computer he develops a feeling for its behaviour under various circumstances and so is led to discover the rules which govern it. Unlike instructional CAL where the focus is on the subject material and the aim is to optimise the learner's mastery of it, this form concentrates much more on the pupil and his relationship with the subject as portrayed by the computer.

The use of simulations (and, as we shall see later, model building) is a powerful CAL technique which exploits some of the unique features of the computer as an aid to learning. It enables the pupil to experiment with situations which would otherwise be too expensive, too time consuming or impossibly dangerous. It is possible to think of numerous instances, particularly in the natural and social sciences, where it would be educationally useful, yet usually impractical, for the pupil to have some particular experience. Unlike instructional CAL, where there is usually some other means of administering the subject material, there is often no convenient alternative to the use of a computer based simulation.

**Problems of Simulations**

It is important to realise that in using computer based simulations for learning the intention is to overcome obstacles such as time, cost or danger, which get between the learner and his understanding or feeling for the underlying theory or concepts. In part, this can be achieved by heightening the pupil's involvement with the simulation – a key factor in this form of CAL - so that he will use his imagination to add in missing details. However, care must be taken to ensure that the orderly model presented in the simulation does not so oversimplify the reality it sets out to explicate that it defeats its own object. When they are used to circumvent experimental difficulties simulations do not enable the pupil to acquire experimental skills and so, unless these skills are not required, CAL must remain as a complement to, and not as a replacement for, real experiments.

A second problem arises from the assumptions that may be made about the pupil's encounter with the revelatory CAL package. The package is usually designed to guide the pupil's investigation of the model along a route which will help him to build the desired concepts of its behaviour. Typically it will assume that the pupil comes fresh to the simulation before discussing it with his peers who may have already worked through the package. This discussion may well preempt the planning and strategy of the package because the pupil can then outguess the package and so avoid parts of the carefully planned progression through the material.

## The Conjectural Paradigm

The use of the educational computer to assist the pupil in his manipulation and testing of ideas and hypotheses is one of the most exciting forms of CAL, but also perhaps the most difficult to explain and comprehend. It is based on the concept that knowledge can be created through the learner's experiences and its emphasis is on the pupil's exploration of information on a particular topic. This exploration is supported by the computer which is firmly under the pupil's control. In its simplest form the computer may be used as a calculator to help work through complicated arithmetic: at its most complex the CAL package can offer sophisticated tools for modelling real life situations or for manipulating ideas. Because in the conjectural form of CAL it is the pupil who is in control of the learning rather than the other way about, he is brought much closer to instructing or programming the computer than in the instructional or revelatory forms. This does not necessarily imply that the pupil and his teachers will tell the computer what to do - program it - with a general purpose programming language. It may be convenient and appropriate to do so, but often it is more satisfactory to provide a simpler means of controlling the computer and one which has been designed specifically for this educational purpose.

One of the criteria which should influence how the pupil communicates with the computer is the degree of familiarity with the machine and its use. We have stressed the dictum that a knowledge of computing and programming skills should not be a prerequisite for successful use of CAL. While this will often lead us away from programming languages that have been designed for programmers, it is not so much a problem when the pupils are already studying computing and programming. Then it may be more convenient and natural for the pupil to use the programming language with which he is already familiar rather than to learn an alternative one, even though the alternative may be couched in educational terms.

## Model Building

The use of the computer as a sophisticated calculating device is rapidly becoming an integral part of school science and technology courses. Therefore it may seem curious to include it under the umbrella of computer assisted learning, or even educational computing. However it can be argued that since the pupil is, or should be, learning from his experience, then it is indeed educational. Moreover the step from using the computer as a calculator to modelling real world systems is relatively small and modelling is certainly a form of CAL. There are many similarities between the processes of simulation used in revelatory CAL and the modelling found in conjectural CAL. Both are concerned with using the computer to evaluate some system, process or phenomena so that its behaviour may be investigated and or predicted. A useful practical

**33**

distinction is that of the control over the internal working which is given to the pupil. A pupil using a CAL simulation may be encouraged to change its external conditions but is prevented from altering (or sometimes even examining) the equations which control its behaviour. On the other hand, in modelling, the pupil can be asked to specify some parts of the model or to construct the model and then examine its behaviour and see how well it conforms to the real world. Thus the pupil is able to formulate and test hypotheses about the system he is studying.

As we have already seen, it was to be expected that this form of CAL would find a ready acceptance in many science and technology subjects because in these areas the use of the computer is taken more for granted and modelling does not appear to be anything out of the ordinary. For example, a pupil studying physics might interact with a computer program which modelled the behaviour of a transistor, to compare his experimental results with those obtained from the model and to comment on any disparities. While this exercise requires a knowledge of semiconductor physics it is not a very demanding programming task and it is reasonable to expect that pupils with some programming experience would have few problems in tackling it.

In an environment where the pupils are not familiar with computers and their programming it is possible to devise special programs which will facilitate their dialogue with the computer and allow them to build and investigate their own models. This idea has been used with some success in teaching concepts of geometry and shape to young children. The child can instruct the computer to draw lines on the screen of his computer terminal or on a sheet of paper. He controls the length of the lines and after each line can instruct the computer to change direction before drawing the next. Thus by giving the instructions to draw a line of unit length and then to turn right through ninety degrees a total of four times, the child can obtain the trace of a square. Similar sequences will produce other polygons. By experimentation the child can create a wide variety of patterns and through this experience create his own knowledge of shapes. In the process he will also learn something about problem solving and how to use a computer, but this can be thought of as a useful byproduct.

The concept of hypothesis building and testing is not restricted to mathematics and science, but can also be used in less obvious subjects such as history. The study of local history particularly at secondary level can involve the manipulation of large amounts of data gleaned from parish registers, commercial directories, census returns and so on. From various pieces of evidence in this store of facts the pupil is asked to draw some conclusions, to look for additional confirmation and to investigate the limits of his conclusion, that is, to see how far the evidence can be squeezed and where the evidence is too flimsy to support any further inferences. The historical hypothesising can be supported by using the computer to store all the historical data and then to retrieve the relevant facts requested by the pupil historian. Although the necessary computer programs are quite complex, they can be made quite easy to use and so, once the programs have been made available, there is no need for the teacher or his pupils to become proficient programmers.

Possibly the most exciting, but as yet the least developed, form of conjectural CAL is based on sophisticated artificial intelligence programs and intelligent knowledge based systems (IKBS) which allow the pupil to manipulate a wide variety of concepts and to explore logical frameworks. The programs required are derived from research into artificial intelligence and this is partly responsible for the underveloped state of this form of CAL - it must follow the state of the artificial intelligence art and it is only now that these techniques are becoming viable teaching tools.

## The Emancipatory Paradigm

The fourth and last of the CAL paradigms concerns the use of the computer as a means of reducing the work load of the pupil. For example, the pupil may need to carry out some extensive calculations to obtain the final results from an experiment. While it may be useful for the pupil to have additional practice at these calculations the important feature of the experiment is the final result - the calculations are not a valued part of the learning experience. Similarly, in the local history example described above, it would be possible for the pupil to search through all the available data for the relevant evidence, but the mechanics of the search would take considerable time and would not necessarily contribute to his hypothesis, its formation and testing. The computer is a machine which excels at rapid, accurate calculation and information handling, and is a very suitable means of reducing the amount of inauthentic labour in the learning process, supporting the pupil by providing him with facilities for calculation, information retrieval and so on. As we will see later, it can also be used to support the teacher and trainer in the management of learning.

The teacher must decide the extent to which the labour involved in a particular learning task is authentic or inauthentic. It may play an important role in encouraging the pupil to think about the problem in a creative way. While it is true that the calculations at the end of a practical experiment or the manual extraction of historical evidence from a mass of data does not contribute directly to the learning, they may provide valuable practice in skills which the pupil will need later. Scientists and engineers need to be able to carry out calculations and historians need to know how to search through census returns and commercial directories, if only so that they will be able to produce the relevant computer programs if need be. We should not become dependent on the omniscient computer. There may also be resistance from the pupils themselves who have traditionally seen the inauthentic labour as an integral and essential part of the learning task. Thus, carrying out the calculation is in some way a confirmation of the learning they have got from the experiment. If this prop is removed, even though the teacher believes that the underlying principles are thus made more visible, then the pupils may suspect the value of the learning task.

## Serendipity Learning

The use of the computer to support a pupil's browsing - what might be called computer assisted serendipity - also falls conveniently within this paradigm. The computer could be used to store large quantities of information structured in such a way as to facilitate enquiries on various individual and related topics. It can be programmed to respond on being asked questions, either by regurgitating the relevant prestored facts or by indicating the whereabouts of the appropriate sources of information. The structuring of the information within the computer can allow the pupil to explore a particular subject in depth or move to associated topics. The mass of raw information and the cross linking necessary to support the browsing activity is vast and unless the topics are severely restricted, needs phenomenal resources to set up before the system is fully usable.

In practice the emancipatory form of CAL usually appears as an adjunct to another use and it may be difficult to decide which of the forms predominates. Many of the CAL applications described above, for example the simulations in social science and biology, the retrieval of information from a mass of historical data and the calculations involved in modelling a real world system, could be carried out without the use of a computer, relying on manual, inauthentic labour for their computations: some of course, would be quite impractical, given the timescale of the learning process. Often the teacher is attracted by a characteristic of just one of the four types of CAL. This can then provide the trigger for the change in curriculum or teaching methods. Then other advantages can be exploited and the new learning package may contain features of different kinds of CAL, appropriately combined and further complemented by other non-CAL teaching media.

## The Rationale for CAL

Each of the four types of CAL exploits various features of the computer to assist in the teaching and learning process and, in particular, uses the computer to provide learning opportunities which would be difficult or impractical to provide in any other way. Thus, in the instructional form, the computer is used as a patient tutor; in the revelatory form it is used to mediate between the learner and a hidden model or simulation of a real world situation; in the conjectural form it helps the learner to formulate and test his hypotheses; in the emancipatory form it reduces the amount of nonessential work he must do to reach his learning objectives. In all its forms it can provide a more active partner for the pupil in his pursuit of learning than would be possible with other teaching media such as books, programmed instruction texts, tape slide and the like.

At the same time the pupil can feel that he is only exposing his learning problems and weaknesses to a machine which in some way does not matter, rather than to his teacher or his peers who do. So in addition to the possibilities of individualising instruction, the pupil can feel protected from his mistakes rather than exposed by them and encouraged to experiment with fewer inhibitions.

CAL may be perceived as optimising the pupil's performance towards prespecified goals - the use of a technology of education to centre the course on the subject material, or seen as a way of optimising the instruction towards the pupil's own goals - the use of technology in education to centre the course firmly on the pupil. We should be clear as to the aim of our use of the technology in any given situation. To return to a recurrent theme of this paper, we must be careful to distinguish between the value of the technology and the value of the learning that we seek to facilitate by its use. If CAL is to be used effectively, then it must be used appropriately, that is where it offers learning opportunities which could not easily be provided in any other way.

## Using Computer Based Learning

In the previous section we discussed the various ways in which CAL could assist in the learning process and concluded that, if it was to be used appropriately and hence effectively, it should be used to provide teaching and learning which could not easily be made available by other means. This section is concerned with the production of CAL packages and their integration into the curriculum and the teaching learning process.

CAL, like other educational technologies and teaching methods, has various unique qualities and should be seen in the context of alternative methods of learning, each of which has its own useful qualities. It is one, but only one, of the tools that the teacher can use to help with his teaching and learning problems. It follows therefore that CAL will be one but only one, of the components of a complete learning package. Typically it will support, or be supported by, printed materials and conventional lessons or tutorials; sometimes it may be used in conjunction with other non-book media. There are three reasons for using a variety of media;

- appropriate use;
- financial constraints; and
- variety.

As we have seen, each medium should be used appropriately to obtain the greatest benefit from it. For example, the background information required by the pupil prior to carrying out a CAL simulation could be presented as part of the CAL program on the pupil's terminal or could be printed as a set of notes which the pupil could study away from the terminal. It may be more appropriate to adopt the latter approach rather than to use the computer as an automated page turner. Secondly, the appropriate use of technology is bound by financial constraints. While printed material is relatively cheap, the use of CAL is admittedly expensive and therefore must be deployed with care so as to be cost effective. At the same time, teachers are also very expensive and they too must be employed appropriately. Finally, the variety obtained by using a combination of different media and teaching styles can help to retain the pupil's enthusiasm and interest in his learning. A course which consists only of a series of CAL programs where the pupil interacts only with a computer terminal, could be as boring as a course based only on didactic presentations where the pupil sits with a score or so of his peers listening to a teacher at the opposite end of a classroom.

## Print Media

Books and pupil notes are cheap to produce or buy and are durable. They do not require any special equipment for their use (except by the blind or partially sighted) and, being small and portable, can be used almost anywhere. They are reliable in that they do not go wrong and even if damaged, for example by having coffee spilled on them, they are still usable. However, they are passive aids to learning; the pupil may respond to the book but the book cannot detect whether the pupil is having difficulty with a particular topic and modify its approach to try a different strategy. With careful design, a programmed instruction text may go some way towards alleviating this problem, but the printed word remains essentially passive and static.

## Tape Slide

The combination of tape and slide is also a passive medium but one which gives a large information bandwidth; in other words the pupil can receive information at a fast rate by looking at pictures and listening. The use of sound recording also allows the author to inject more variety and realism into the presentation. The sound track can thus include recordings of different people and situations instead of printed quotations and word pictures. The costs are higher than for printed materials and although the technique requires some equipment, this can be made relatively simple and reliable. Although it is portable, it is inconvenient to use it away from the normal classroom. It is more sensitive to damage than printed materials.

## Video

Video recorded and film material offer further improvements in the speed and quality of presentation of material. The animation affords greater impact on the audience and the means of explaining moving phenomena. But the costs of production and delivery are much greater than for printed materials or tape slide. The equipment is more complex and less reliable and is also not portable, so that it is confined to a given study area. Although the learner can view a particular sequence an unlimited number of times, the medium is still passive because it cannot respond differently to each pupil or vary its approach to take account of a pupil's individual problems.

## Teachers

Teachers are very versatile teaching devices. Their outstanding ability is their adaptability which even for a poor teacher potentially exceeds that of the best adaptive CAL package. A teacher is able to sense and probe a pupil's learning difficulties and then to try a succession of different strategies, either singly or in combination, in an attempt to overcome the problem. Moreover, the teacher can learn from his previous encounters with pupils and the subject material and so evolve new methods of presentation. The teacher is versatile and, while his specialism may be limited to one or two broad subject areas, he can teach a large number of topics within those areas. He can usually also teach a much wider range of subjects at lower levels. The teacher is largely self programming, in that he can prepare his own lessons with the minimum of external support from an educational development unit or audiovisual production team. Teachers can operate with unsophisticated equipment, such as a blackboard and chalk or an overhead projector, but will often use these only as ancilliaries and most can, if necessary, teach without any extra equipment at all. They are easy to produce but difficult to train and once in use are expensive to keep. Intelligence, adaptability and versatility have their price. Since the training of a teacher takes several years, there is a considerable delay between the realisation that demand is increasing and the response of an increased supply. Teachers are reliable but prone to minor failures or illnesses which may render them inoperative or less efficient for a few days.

However, while teachers are the most effective all round teaching devices they do have some drawbacks to offset their many virtues. Because of their high cost their availability is limited, so that it is not usually possible to have just a few pupils for each teacher. The teacher's ability to adjust his teaching to the needs of individual pupils, and hence his effectiveness, can be seriously diluted in large classes. The problem is compounded by the administrative load which inevitably falls on our teachers and reduces the time that they can devote to their pupils. This may be alleviated by using the computer to assist with the management of learning. The second drawback is the teacher's limited presentation bandwidth. Although the teacher is very adapable, by himself he can only impart information to his pupils by speech and gestures. This makes it difficult for him to explain visual phenomena or the functioning of dynamic systems, unless he makes use of other media to support these parts of the course. Thirdly, because his speed of calculation is limited, the teacher's explication of real world systems may have to be calculated and hence is less flexible.

## Computers

Computers are less flexible devices for supporting learning than teachers but they are nevertheless a great improvement on other media. Their key feature is their ability to process information, to carry out calculations and to mediate in the flow of information between the learner and his learning environment quickly and accurately. This ability can be used to provide the pupil with an infinitely patient tutor, to simulate and model real world systems with textual or animated diagrammatic output, or to reduce the amount of inessential labour involved in the pupil's learning. But CAL is not a universal panacea for all learning problems. It requires expensive equipment which is only semiportable. The equipment is complex and so not completely reliable. The CAL materials are not easily damaged (damage in this context is rather different from the sort of damage that might be done to a book or video tape) but even slight damage will make the program unusable. CAL's main drawback is its cost, which falls somewhere between the low cost of printed material and the high cost of individual or small group tuition.

## The Multimedia Package

Thus we come to the concept of a learning package which consists of a number of different contributions to a specific topic, using a variety of media in an appropriate combination. It is often argued that the use of CAL replaces the teacher with technology and thus dehumanises the learning process. This is certainly true of any attempt to replace the teacher, whether it be by CAL, educational television or the exclusive use of programmed learning, and it is unquestionably undesirable. Education is essentially a social process involving interaction between human beings. However, a central thesis is that CAL should be used appropriately to complement rather than to replace the teacher. The multimedia package will therefore usually include a contribution from the teacher as well as from the computer. In those cases where CAL is the dominant component, the whole may be regarded as a CAL package. The package is sometimes referred to by CAL practitioners as "courseware", forming a triad with its computing partners "hardware" and "software".

## Producing CAL Packages

There is much similarity between the production of CAL packages and of packages involving other media. The production process starts with specification of the educational or training objectives of the whole package and is followed by the overall design of the package.

It is at this stage that the designer must be aware of the strengths and weaknesses of the various techniques and resources at his disposal so that he can make informed decisions about the complementary roles of each of the different contributions. He must specify the objectives and the strategy of each contribution and thus determine, in the case of the CAL program, the blend of the different forms of CAL (instructional, revelatory, conjectural, emancipatory) that will be used. From this overall design can come the detailed design of the individual contributions, including the CAL program.

In the previous section we discussed various kinds of CAL from an education viewpoint. Now we should consider the different ways in which the pupil can interact with the computer and use the CAL program. These present major implications for the educational strategy which is to be used, but are also constrained by practical considerations of what is technically feasible and available in the right place at the right time.

**Presenting CAL Packages**

The traditional picture of CAL in most people's minds is that of a pupil seated in front of a computer terminal, reading messages displayed on the screen of the terminal or typed out on a roll of paper, and typing his responses on a keyboard rather like that of an ordinary typewriter. This is also the most common way of giving pupils access to the computer but is not necessarily the most effective in all circumstances. Both alphameric and graphics terminals are standard pieces of computing equipment - although this does not imply that they are widely available in educational and training institutions. There have been a number of projects in various countries to develop a special purpose terminal for CAL which could handle a number of different media, all under computer control, at one pupil learning station. The computer can instruct the terminal to print a certain character or to draw a line in a certain photographic slide or microfiche image, to play a certain sound recording on a tape recorder, control a video cassette or videodisk, or to synthesise a short verbal message to the pupil. In general these multi-media terminals have not been widely used because of their greater cost and because of the educational complexity in designing effective teaching packages that will use the facilities. However, there are strong indications that interactive video will prove an exception.

Perhaps we should ask whether it is reasonable that the development of keyboard skills should be a part of our pupils' basic training, as other study techniques are. It is at least arguable that typing is an artificial impediment, imposed only by some computer based methods of teaching and training.

As indicated previously, the traditional picture of CAL has a single pupil sitting at each terminal so that the computer acts as a mediator between the pupil and his learning environment. While it may be the most suitable arrangement for instructional CAL it provides a very solitary, if individualised, environment for the pupil. In many circumstances, in revelatory and conjectural CAL, it is advantageous for pupils to work in small groups. Educationally this can enrich the CAL lesson, because the pupils can now discuss their progress with each other and so help each other with their problems,

**41**

understanding and hypotheses. The pupils can learn as much, if not more, from their dialogue together, as from the supportive CAL package which may recede into a more passive role, prompting the pupils and verifying their hypotheses. A major factor in the cost of CAL is the provision of computer equipment and an arrangement where pupils work together on a CAL package and can give substantial savings in the computing resources required.

## Structuring the Material

There are direct parallels between the detailed design of a CAL package and the design of packages using other media. The designer must start with a clear understanding of what, educationally, the package is required to do, and then keep these educational objectives clearly in view while exploiting the strengths and circumventing the weaknesses of each medium. Whereas the designer of a programmed instruction text is working with printed words and diagrams, and the designer of a tape slide sequence operates with a commentary and a set of pictures, the CAL author is producing a structured series of short dialogues between the pupils or pupils and the computer, perhaps augmented with diagrams that will be displayed on the terminal and other materials such as printed pupil notes. The dialogue is not spoken, but printed on the terminal and typed by the pupil; this has implications for the phraseology in the same way that a written commentary can sound stilted when it is spoken on a tape.

A significant difference between CAL and many other media is the ability of a CAL package to break out of a linear sequence of material to recap or offer an alternative approach, to allow the pupil to change something in his model or simulation and to respond to his individual preferences. This requires that the package material be very carefully structured so that the pupil can follow a sensible path through the lesson. There are probably an infinite number of different ways in which pupils could study a particular topic but it is not possible to devise a package which will explicitly allow for all of the possible permutations. The skill of the CAL author lies in structuring a package so that it will satisfy most of the pupils for most of the time, while remaining of manageable size and complexity.

## The CAL Production Team

The sheer quantity of dialogue and structure in many CAL packages poses production problems which different authors and authorities have sought to overcome in different ways:

- by providing specialist CAL authors;
- by encouraging teachers to produce their own materials;
- by setting up hybrid production teams.

One school of thought says that the actual production of the material should be undertaken by a CAL specialist who can take a detailed educational design from the teacher and turn it into a draft package. Another advocates that facilities should be made available for teachers to produce their own materials. The first group argue that it is wasteful for teachers to develop the production and programming skills necessary to write and check the sequences of instructions to the computer; it is much more efficient for this process to be handled by a specialist author who is very familiar with the techniques required and any problems that may be encountered. This argument is countered by the second group who point out that the cost of employing a specialist is a luxury many authorities cannot afford and who maintain that it is possible for teachers to carry out the work themselves, if they are provided with the necessary tools. They claim that it is preferable for the teacher to have the detailed knowledge and control over the package which is possible if he himself produces it. As with the production of other media, both sides can be right in different circumstances; the choice depends on the complexity of the package, the level of specialist support available and the proficiency of the teacher.

## Evaluation

As we have seen, the appropriate and most effective applications of CAL are in areas which exploit the unique qualities of the medium. CAL can often provide learning opportunities which are very different from those which would be found in a course taught by other means; sometimes there are parts of the course which would be impractical without the use of a CAL simulation or some other form of computer support. Hence it can be misleading to carry out a quantitative comparison between the learning resulting from a CAL package and from, say, a conventional lesson or laboratory exercise. Any comparison should examine the qualitative aspects of using CAL as a component in the package, to determine whether CAL is the best educational tool to use in the given circumstances.

# COMPUTER LANGUAGES AND LEARNING

Bill Finzer and Diane Resek

## A Classroom Scene

In the back of the third year classroom, three pupils are seated in front of the computer. "Let's see what the whole dance looks like so far," says one. The pupil at the keyboard types **DOIT** and presses the **RETURN** key. To their delight a funny little bald-headed man on the screen winks at them twice, does a shuffle to the left and leaps back to the right.

**Figure I: The dancer leaps across the screen to his left**

"For the next step, he could kick first one leg and then the other," the girl in the middle says as she puts down the manual and gets up to demonstrate. "We'll just call it **'TO KICK'** ".

Referring to an instruction page with pictures of the dancer's possible legs, they work out the sequence of commands to define the **KICK** routine.

TO KICK

LEFTLEG 2

LEFTLEG 1

RIGHTLEG 2

RIGHTLEG 1

END

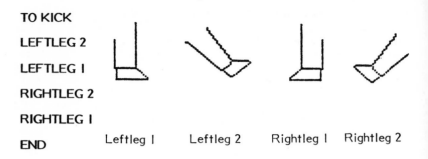

Leftleg 1     Leftleg 2     Rightleg 1     Rightleg 2

**Figure 2: The pupils' definition of TO KICK**

As they type each command and press **RETURN**, the dancer on the screen obediently responds by moving the appropriate leg.

Before the pupils defined it, **KICK** was not a word that the dancer could respond to. Now, **KICK** stands for a routine and is a part of the dancer's vocabulary. The pupils go on to define several more steps and to try putting their steps together in several different ways to create their finished dance. They **SAVE** all their work on a disk so that later in the day they can show their teacher and some of the other pupils what they did.

The pupils in the above scene have never programmed a computer before, nor in their minds are they programming one now. They think about their work as creating a dance. But a choreographed dance has much in common with a computer program; each step in a dance corresponds to an instruction in a program; each routine in a dance corresponds to a procedure or subroutine in a program. Although they may not be aware of it, the pupils *are* programming; that is, they are writing a sequence of instructions which the computer follows.

Ten years ago very few people were in sufficiently intimate contact with a computer to realise that there was such a thing as a program that determined what the computer did; fewer still had any idea how to write a program. Today, as microcomputers enter more and more homes, classrooms, and offices, many people have the concept of a computer program, but the process of programming is seen as esoteric and difficult, something quite different from what we normally do. Special courses are being created at every level from primary school to postgraduate study to teach people how to program.

However, there are many activities in our daily lives that are analogous to programming: giving a friend directions to get to a house; writing down a recipe for a special dish; explaining to a housesitter how to care for one's plants. None of these processes needs to be difficult and neither does programming. Why then should so many people's first experiences in programming be fraught with difficulty?

**46**

We have used the dancer described above with primary school children and adult learners as an easy, first experience with programming computers. The next section explores some reasons why the dancer *does* work as an introduction to programming. However, our main interests centre on finding ways to use computers to teach specific subject matter. At present, when we look at computers in schools we find they are most commonly used as drill and practice machines, expensive substitutes for textbooks, and purveyors of video games. The exploration of the dancer language will lead us to discover ways that computers can be used to teach other subject matter, ways that are significantly better than the ones we usually find in schools now.

The first reason that the dancer works as an introduction to programming is that nearly all of the dancer's commands cause something to happen on the screen. As soon as the pupil types **LEFTLEG 2** and presses the **RETURN** key, the dancer's left leg actually moves. Furthermore, the thing that happens - motion, change of expression, change of body part - is directly related to the goal at hand, which is to create a dance. Lastly, most people find the goal of creating a dance an accessible one and one that is interesting, at least for an hour or so, which is all they usually need in order to learn the useful lessons about programming that the dancer language embodies.

Let us compare what it is like to be introduced to programming through the dancer with what it is like to begin with a standard programming language like BASIC. We see first that very few BASIC commands (usually only printing commands) cause something to happen immediately on the screen; most have to do with manipulating values of variables inside the computer's memory or with controlling the order of execution of the commands that make up the program. Therefore, an extra level of abstraction is introduced into the programming process which makes understanding what is going on more difficult. To further complicate matters, when one actually programs, nothing at all happens on the screen (beyond the appearance of typed characters) until the program is **RUN.**

Although the dancer language is extremely limited, its limitations are an advantage for beginners in that almost any effect they wish to produce is accomplished very directly from the available commands. The learner feels in control of the constrained world made available by the language. In contrast, more complete languages quickly raise expectations to a level beyond that which is immediately accessible by the commands provided. For example, working with BASIC, a novice may think it should be easy to teach the computer to play tic-tac-toe, but soon finds that even though the game is simple for humans, the computer program is surprisingly complex and consists of a tremendous number of steps. People can, of course, master the art of constructing large effects from very small steps. The dancer language serves as a satisfying introduction to this process. After several hours of programming with the dancer, the beginner is ready to move on to a larger language with some confidence in their ability to learn to program.

## Alternatives to General Purpose Programming Languages

Before we proceed further, let us consider why it is that we want to teach programming to anyone besides those relatively few people who are going to become programmers or computer scientists. The usual response to this question is that we wish to give people as much control over the computer as they will need, and true control comes with the ability to program. People need control because there is never exactly the right piece of software to do what they want, and so, if they can program (and have the time), they can create their own software.

An alternative to courses which teach general purpose programming languages emerges as a result of looking at easy introductions to programming, such as the dancer language. One begins to wonder if most people might be better off learning programming concepts in particular subject-matter courses like chemistry, geometry, or music. The trouble with programming languages like BASIC or PASCAL in this regard, is that they do not come equipped to deal with entities like molecules or triangles, or concepts like interest rate and musical phrase. In the sections that follow we explore what it might mean if particular 'sub-languages' *did* come with such higher-level concepts embedded in them. The flexibility of these sub-languages would allow one to create, in a subject matter environment, the exact piece of software that is needed. At the same time, the sub-languages would be so compatible with the subject matter that students could learn to program in a natural way as they explore the content areas.

## Languages with Subject Matter Content

The main reason for using the dancer in a course is to introduce programming; however, pupils may learn other concepts as well. For example, using the dancer language, a pupil easily moves the dancer **UP, DOWN, RIGHT,** and **LEFT** on the screen, where **LEFT** and **RIGHT** are from the dancer's point of view. We might find that for a particular pupil, say in the infant school, part of the learning that is going on involves understanding the meaning of these words and being able to put herself into the dancer's body. Let us agree that for such a child, part of the 'subject matter content' of the dancer language is the concept of the four directions as seen by the dancer. Thus, an infant can learn to write programs in the dancer language while learning other content.

BASIC, though not a sub-language, can be thought of as having subject matter content also. BASIC makes it easy to do arithmetic. We can add, subtract, multiply, divide, and raise to a power almost effortlessly; we do not need to teach the computer how to do these things when we are programming in BASIC. Furthermore, when we ask the computer to evaluate an expression like

$$2 + 3 * 4$$

the computer does the multiplication before the addition and comes up with 14 rather than 20; that is, it uses normal algebraic 'precedence rules'. For beginning pupils who are not yet familiar with these precedence rules, writing simple arithmetic programs in BASIC will, in part, help them to learn algebraic precedence. Algebraic precedence is part of the subject matter content of BASIC; indeed, BASIC programming has been used successfully as part of beginning algebra courses to help children learn algebra(1).

But neither the dancer language nor BASIC has much relevance to a chemistry, geometry, or music course. The subject matter content of each of these courses is quite dissimilar or remote from the content of BASIC. However, we can imagine, or even design, languages that *would* be relevant to these courses.

One of the fundamentally important consequences of the programmability of the computer is that computers can be taught to understand new languages. If this were not the case, then we would always be forced to communicate with the computer in its native machine language. It has been a primary goal of computer scientists, ever since the invention of the computer, to teach it to communicate in ever 'higher' or more 'natural' languages. Modern high-level programming languages are still far removed from English: their syntax is simpler and far more rigid and their vocabulary is much more limited.

But even if the computer cannot understand all of English, it can be made to respond to at least some of the vocabulary of a subject area, like music or geometry. If this is done, then some of the content of the subject matter will have been introduced into a programming language. Such languages, can be used, as BASIC is used to help teach algebra, in these different subject matter courses. In the following sections we introduce some special purpose languages which do just that. None of the languages discussed is a fully general programming language; that is, you cannot do all the things that you could do with BASIC or PASCAL. So, we call them 'sub-languages' to remind ourselves of this fact.

### Turtle Talk, a Sub-Language for Geometry

In 1968, Seymour Papert and the MIT Logo group (2) began extending the Logo language so that it could address a small robot connected to a computer. The robot, called a 'turtle', moved around on large sheets of paper covering the floor and had a pen that could be used to draw lines as it moved. Later versions of the language used a simulated turtle which appeared in the form of a small triangle on the computer screen. As the triangle moved, its 'pen' would leave a line behind it on the screen showing its path. Papert called the sub-language of Logo that dealt with the turtle, 'Turtle Talk'.

**49**

Typing commands to the turtle in order to draw interesting pictures on the screen is similar to directing the dancer. The program for the finished picture corresponds to the program for the complete dance; the routines that make up the dance correspond to procedures to draw parts of the picture. The subject matter content of Turtle Talk is geometry, which corresponds to the rather limited dance content of the dancer language.

## The Power of Defining Your Own Words

"There's glory from you!"
"I don't know what you mean by 'glory,' " Alice said.
Humpty Dumpty smiled contemptuously. "Of course you don't - till I tell you. I meant 'there's a nice knock-down argument for you!' "
"But 'glory' doesn't mean 'a nice knock-down argument,' " Alice objected.
"When I use a word," Humpty Dumpty said, in rather a scornful tone, "it means just what I choose it to mean - neither more nor less."
"The question is," said Alice, "whether you can make words mean so many different things."
"The question is," said Humpty Dumpty, "which is to be master - that's all."

Lewis Carroll, *Through the Looking Glass*

The three pupils in our classroom scene, in defining the **KICK** routine, defined a new word in the dancer's vocabulary. Whereas before, the dancer would respond to **KICK** with an error message complaining that it didn't understand what **KICK** meant, now **KICK** will cause the dancer first to raise and lower his left and then his right leg. Languages such as the dancer language are called 'extensible', meaning that new words can be defined in them. BASIC is an example of a 'non-extensible' language in that only the words that come with the language can be used in a program. PASCAL and LOGO, on the other hand, are extensible.

Now it is a very powerful thing to be able to define the meaning of new words within a language. The pupil says to the computer, "This is what I mean by **HEXAGON**". The pupil becomes an insider in the subject area, a geometer doing geometry.

In this manner the computer provides motivation for learning geometrical definitions and theorems. In learning the traditional middle school geometry, pupils are expected to memorize definitions and theorems. Their only motivation comes from being told they will need it later on. Using Turtle Talk, pupils can discover their own operational definition of a word such as 'hexagon' by trying to teach the turtle to draw a certain kind of picture. Now the pupils feel as if they own the word. They are its masters and no longer slaves to a textbook definition.

**50**

## Symmetry, Music and Rubik's Cube

BASIC can be useful in teaching algebra, and Turtle Talk can help students learn geometry. These are not unique examples of learning subject matter through sub-languages. In Figure 3 the special vocabularies for three languages in different subject areas are listed. We will examine briefly each of these languages and their subject matter content.

| Symmetry | Music | Rubik's Cube |
|---|---|---|
| FORWARD | DO, RE, MI | U, D, R, L, F, B |
| LEFT | FA, SO, LA, TI | |
| MULTIPLYBY | WHOLE, HALF, | |
| | QUARTER, EIGHTH | |
| | SIXTEENTH | |

Figure 3: Vocabularies for three sub-languages

*Symmetry*

In a geometry unit for middle school children we wished to introduce the topic of symmetry. Turtle Talk by itself does not allow one to create symmetric designs very easily, therefore another command was added to Turtle Talk, **MULTIPLYBY**, whose action is to turn a single turtle on the screen into a number of turtles pointing symmetrically outwards around the location of the original turtle. The new turtles respond in unison to any additional Turtle Talk commands, and in doing so, rapidly create interesting designs along with a rotational symmetry determined by the number of turtles. Figure 4 shows one such design and the program which produced it.

```
TO HOOK
FORWARD 40
LEFT 135
FORWARD 40
END
MULTIPLYBY 8
HOOK
```

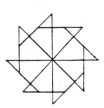

Figure 4: Program showing rotational symmetry

Using the expanded language, pupils discover properties of symmetrical designs. For example, they find that if they turn the resulting design through an angle of 360 degrees divided by the rotational symmetry (45 degrees for the design in Figure 4) the design will remain unchanged.

*Music*

In the Music sub-language, the commands **DO, RE, MI, FA, SO, LA,** and **TI** produce the notes of the scale. The octave of the note is specified by a number so that **RE 3** produces a note in the third octave of the computer's range. The commands **WHOLE, HALF, QUARTER, EIGHT,** and **SIXTEENTH** determine the duration of the note. Pupils compose music by first creating phrases and then putting the phrases together to make songs. In addition to hearing the sounds, the notes appear on a musical staff. An even richer language would result from including commands to change the time signature, transpose to a different key, change the tempo, add harmonies, play melodies backwards, and so on.

*Rubik's Cube*

In using the Rubik's Cube sub-language one 'talks' to the cube itself, manipulating it with the commands, **U, D, R, L, F** and **B** which turn the up, down, right, left, front and back faces respectively a quarter-turn clockwise. A picture on the screen shows the current state of the cube. The special benefit the computer languages provides is a sequence of individual moves that can be combined together into one single routine. The properties of these more complex moves can then be explored. So here is a situation in which the sub-language makes it easy for pupils to explore a very narrow, but rich content area, namely the workings of a particular puzzle.

**Languages With Variables**

All the sub-languages we have discussed so far have been extensible, thereby giving pupils the power to define new words. We have discussed the positive effect on learning issuing from that power. However, these languages have serious limitations. Suppose that a pupil wishes to make several hexagons of different sizes on the screen. The **HEXAGON** routine produces a hexagon of side forty units. Should a separate **HEXAGON** routine be written for *each* size hexagon needed? Logo's Turtle Talk allows the pupil to define *one* routine which will produce any size hexagon desired. One way to write that routine is as follows:

```
TO HEXAGON :SIZE
REPEAT 6 FORWARD :SIZE LEFT 60
END
```

Now the command **HEXAGON** must be followed by a number to indicate the size of hexagon to be drawn. For example,

```
HEXAGON 10
```

would produce a hexagon of side 10 units.

Variables are not just useful in mathematically oriented languages like Turtle Talk. The need for a variable arises in the context of the Music sub-language and in nearly all other sub-languages also. If a pupil wishes to hear a given musical phrase in a different key or at a different tempo, the phrase can be defined in terms of two variables: key and tempo. The same phrase can be used in different compositions or in different ways within one composition by changing the key, the tempo, or both. This capability enriches the possibilities for pupils' musical explorations. In the next section we examine two examples of sub-languages where the use of variables is central to exploring the subject matter.

### In-Out Machines as an Introduction to Elementary Algebra

Back in the classroom, this time a hypothetical second year mathematics class; three pupils and a computer are working on the task of creating an in-out machine. An in-out machine takes some input, usually a number, and uses a rule to determine what will be done with the input to produce the machine's output, which also is usually a number. In-out machines have been used for a long time to introduce the concept of a function (3). What is unique about the interaction below is that the pupils are creating their own in-out machine using a sub-language we call 'Easy Speak'.

"So far," recaps Perry, "whenever the input is odd, the output of the machine will be two times the input. But we haven't said yet what should happen when the input is even."

"Well," suggests Lu, "since the first part of the machine's rule is fairly easy, let's make the second part a bit harder, like maybe use a subtraction rule, like twenty minus the input."

Gerry at the keyboard has just filled in the second condition, **EVEN (INPUT)**, and then types '20 - INPUT' alongside the cue 'OUTPUT = '.

Their screen looks like the one shown in Figure 5.

IN-OUT MACHINE RULES

1.  Condition: **ODD (INPUT)**

    Output = **2 * INPUT**

2.  Condition: **EVEN (INPUT)**

    Output = **20 - INPUT**

**Figure 5:**     **Perry, Lu, and Gerry's In-Out Machine**

Once they have finished defining their in-out machine to themselves and to the computer, the three pupils try it out. After discovering that the machine behaves as expected for the inputs I to 5, they try some large inputs and an input of zero.

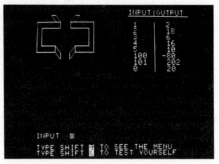

**Figure 6:** **The results of the pupils' trial inputs for their in-out machine**

Satisfied with their work, Perry, Lu, and Gerry save the rules for their newly created machine on a disk. They wish next to see how difficult their in-out machine is for other children in the class to work out. Another group of pupils at the other computer in the room have also finished defining their own in-out machine. The classroom teachers asks the groups to exchange computers and try to discover the rule for the other group's in-out machine by giving trial inputs and observing the outputs.

Easy Speak, when used to build in-out machines, is quite a different programming language from the dancer language or its relatives. It is not extensible, and the need for sequential thinking has gone - it does not matter in what order the rules for the machine are laid out. Nevertheless, the children are programming, without necessarily being aware of it; that is, they are instructing the computer how to react to numbers that are typed in. The pupils creating the machine cannot anticipate all the numbers other pupils will input. For the other pupils to completely understand the machine, they, themselves, should be able to write the rules for the machine in Easy Speak.

What subject matter content do children explore with Easy Speak? They are able to see, manipulate, and create algebraic functions. The functions, as they are embodied in in-out machines, take on a concreteness, a life of their own.

The use of in-out machines has helped pupils to understand functions in many classrooms without computers. What the computer adds to the activity is that once pupils have a function in mind, they are forced to describe their function using a variable **INPUT** and algebraic symbols. In the past, it has been difficult to introduce algebra since its real-world uses are bound to sophisticated knowledge belonging to particular fields. Most introductory algebra books use artificial word problems such as 'If John is twice as old now as he was fifteen years ago, how old is he?' On the other hand, using in-out machines and Easy Speak, pupils are operating in a realm where the sub-language is a natural tool for characterising their own functions. Being able to create a puzzle for their fellow pupils provides a strong motivation to express those ideas.

## A Language for Game Strategies

*The Game*

Besides using Easy Speak with in-out machines, one can use it to describe strategies for the computer to use in playing a game. Consider the game of 'Matches' (sometimes called 'one-pile Nim'), a simple game that has been used frequently in mathematics classrooms. Twelve match sticks are laid out in a line. There are two players who take turns removing one, two, or three matches. The person who takes the last match wins (Figure 7).

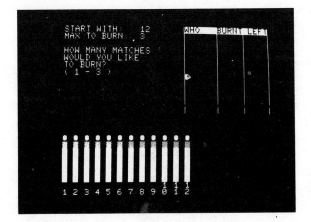

**Figure 7: The twelve match sticks at the start of the game**

*Guess My Strategy*

In the classroom, pupils learn Matches by pairing up and playing with each other. Then, in small groups, they work with a program called 'Guess My Strategy' in which they are pitted against one of the six computer players depicted in Figure 8.

**55**

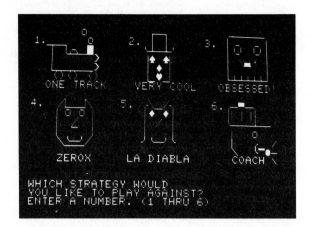

**Figure 8: Picture of the screen showing the 6 strategies**

Each of the computer players has a different strategy for playing Matches. The group's task is to choose one of the players and then determine and describe the strategy for that player. The teacher emphasises that the object is not to *beat* the computer, but to 'psyche it out', to know what it will do in any given circumstance.

The computer strategies are mostly quite simple, and not very effective for winning the game. For example, One Track's strategy is always to take three matches. If given the choice, One Track will want to go first. Zerox, on the other hand, is a copy cat and will always do what the previous player did. Naturally, if given the choice, Zerox would not want to go first.

When the pupils are confident that they understand how a strategy works, they can play the game in 'imitate' mode. They are supposed to *act as though* they were using one of the strategies and are scored on the basis of how closely they were able to imitate it. Usually they discover some aspects of the strategy that they had not thought clearly about, such as when the strategy will wish to go first or when it will wish to go second. The pupils are forced to step outside themselves to see things from another point of view. They must, in some sense, *become* this player inside the computer.

*Programming a Strategy*

Children will tend at first to give rather vague verbal characterisations of strategies for the game of Matches. But when they are told to teach the *computer* so that it has a strategy for playing, they are forced to formulate a particular strategy in a precise language. The listing of figure 9 shows how the pupil would describe a strategy that would take one match except when it is posisble to win, and would always wish to start first.

| | | |
|---|---|---|
| START WITH: | | 12 |
| MAX TO TAKE: | | 3 |
| START CONDITION: | | ALWAYS |
| 1. | CONDITION: | LEFT > 3 |
| | TAKE: | 1 |
| 2. | CONDITION: | LEFT <= 3 |
| | TAKE: | LEFT |

**Figure 9:** A computer strategy for Matches. LEFT is a variable which represents the number of matches left.

Although at first pupils only play Matches starting with twelve matches and with a maximum of three to take, they later try to find strategies for other starting numbers and maxima. Some pupils will want to try to write a 'perfect' strategy using variables for the starting numbers of matches (**START**) and maximum (**MAX**). One version of such a strategy is shown in Figure 10.

| | | |
|---|---|---|
| START WITH: | | START |
| MAX TO TAKE: | | MAX |
| START CONDITION: | | RMD (START, MAX + 1)<>0 |
| 1. | CONDITION: | RMD (LEFT, MAX + 1)<>0 |
| | TAKE: | RMD (LEFT, MAX + 1) |
| 2. | CONDITION: | RMD (LEFT, MAX + 1) = 0 |
| | TAKE: | RANDOM (1, MAX) |

**Figure 10:** A strategy to play Matches perfectly. If the computer does not have a good move, it will take a random number of matches.

What the computer adds to the use of strategy games in the classroom is the facility and motivation for expressing a given strategy precisely. This is another example where computers can be used as a natural tool in the mathematics classroom.

**Programming Integrated Into Content**

We have seen a variety of subject areas that can be enriched using the computer with sub-languages. The learning experience for the pupil is quite different than that produced by the use of drill and practice or CAI programs. As programming languages become ever easier and more natural to use, and more applicable to specific content areas, there will be less and less need for special programming courses except perhaps for students of computer science, in which case, the languages become the content. Programming will become part and parcel of using the computer as a learning tool; but, just as the three pupils working with the dancer in the introduction were not conscious of their programming as such, so learners will be aware mostly of talking to some object on the screen, or making the computer do something.

Computer sub-languages can play the same role in college classrooms **(4)**. Business students in college currently study computer programming in order to be able to use the computer to make sales projections. Business organisations are discovering the usefulness of spreadsheet programs like 'Visi-Calc' and its successors for this purpose. A spreadsheet program provides a special purpose sub-language, which makes it possible for students to use the computer as a tool in the content area course itself, thus obviating the need for a separate programming course. This sub-language serves two purposes. In business courses it is used as a medium for students to explore business concepts. Outside the classroom, it is a general tool for solving business problems in place of relatively inflexible software packages written in standard programming languages.

As programming becomes easier, everyone becomes a programmer without particularly being aware of it. PASCAL and other high-level languages become special purpose languages for doing computer science kinds of things and are used in computer science courses. Each content area, using computers as learning tools, finds the special purpose languages or sub-languages which best suit it. For non-computer science students programming the computer is no longer a subject as such and the need for courses in programming alone disappears.

**Summary and Visions**

Too much of what schools do with computers now is either focused on studying the computers themselves (such as courses which teach computer programming languages) or could be done as well or even better without the computer (as is true with many multiple choice programs). We have discussed methods by which programming and study of particular subject matter can be integrated through the creation of sub-languages with actual content embedded in them. The learner, in using the sub-language to get the computer to do interesting things, learns both about programming and the subject. The computer becomes a tool and the sub-language provides access to a learning environment. The process of learning will no longer be a passive absorbtion of facts, but a creative, active exploration of ideas.

Each new sub-language need not be completely independent of its predecessors. Quite a few of them will share a common syntax as did the dancer language and Turtle Talk, but with different vocabularies. Many of these sub-languages will be embedded in a complete language like Logo. Sub-languages should be easy and natural to learn; they should be interactive so that the pupil obtains as much immediate feedback as possible; they should put the learner in charge of the learning process.

Computers that are now becoming available for use in the classroom have the memory and speed which make possible the development of these kinds of languages. Educators are no longer limited by the hardware, but we shall need the computer science community to provide 'software tools' to make the development of sub-languages easier than it is at present. Perhaps the greatest task will be to convince the educational community and the general public that a role for learners in which they actively explore ideas instead of passively absorb facts is desirable. With these tasks accomplished the potential of the computer to truly improve the kind of learning that takes place in schools and greatly increase its depth may be fulfilled.

## REFERENCES

1.  See, for example, Elgarten, G.H., Posamentier, H.S., and Moresh, S.E., *Using Computers in Mathematics,* Addison-Wesley (1983).

2.  Papert, S., *Mindstorms,* Basic Books (1980).

3.  Davis, R.B., *Explorations in Mathematics,* Addison-Wesley (1967).

4.  See, for example, Roberts et al, *Introduction to Computer Simulation - A System Dynamics Modelling Approach,* Addison-Wesley (1983).

# TEACHING ABOUT COMPUTING

Peter Weston

Where there is no vision, the people perish          Proverbs, 18

## Setting the Scene

The late 1960s and early 1970s saw the introduction of Computer Studies into the school curriculum. There was a proliferation of a variety of courses. Not surprisingly, Examination Boards responded with CSE Mode I and GCE 'O' Level syllabuses and more recently with 'A' Level syllabuses. The increasing popularity of Computer Studies as an examination subject is clearly illustrated by the table below.

| Year | CSE | GCE O level | GCE AO level | GCE A level | CEE | Total |
|------|------|------|------|------|------|------|
| 1977 | 15218 | 6091 | 109 | 1764 | --- | 23182 |
| 1978 | 15489 | 8417 | 511 | 1769 | 233 | 26419 |
| 1979 | 16210 | 11635 | 765 | 2323 | 591 | 31524 |
| 1980 | 17901 | 14907 | 1049 | 2819 | 635 | 37311 |
| 1981 | 23590 | 22546 | 1374 | 3947 | 1250 | 52707 |
| 1982 | 32261 | 37868 | 1524 | 5825 | 1531 | 79009 |

**Figure I: UK Examination Entries for Computer Studies (I)**

Early syllabuses, and unfortunately some of those in use during the early 1980's, resulted in too much emphasis on teaching about *the computer*, and its operation, rather than about computing e.g. concepts and principles of data processing, applications and implications. Practical experience involved pupils writing programs to solve numerical problems. The reasons for this are many and include:

(a)    the background of the mathematicians teaching the subject,

(b)    the lack of pre-service training and commercial experience amongst teachers,

(c)    the type of in-service training provided,

(d)    the problems associated with batch and time-sharing systems used to run pupils' programs,

(e)    dearth of resource materials, for both teacher and pupils, particularly in the areas of applications and implications.

More recently it has been realised that emphasis should be placed on teaching computing through applications. Some of the examination boards have reacted to this realisation. For example, the London Computer Studies 'O'-Level devotes a whole paper to case study. However, we must not concern ourselves solely with examination courses. Until recently, the general tendency has been to provide an examination course for a minority of pupils, thus leaving the majority with little or no experience of computers. This situation is changing as the need to provide *all pupils* with 'computer literacy' is recognised. The approaches I shall be advocating are equally applicable for 'computer literacy' and 'examination courses'. The variables in practice will include the time available, availability of resources, depth of study, etc. The belief underlying my overall strategy is that it is the classroom teacher who ultimately determines the level of success achieved within the classroom. The implication is that if suitable resources (hardware, software, training, print-materials, audio-visual materials, etc.) are not available, then classroom teachers must exert pressure upon those capable of providing them, such as Head Teachers, Local Education Authorities and publishers. The onus is on the teacher to use appropriate resource material supplemented, if necessary, by materials produced personally. There is an ever increasing amount of resource material becoming available for use across the curriculum. Whilst use of this material contributes generally towards the acquisition of computer literacy, it is still important that we ensure adequate provision for all those, pupils and teachers, concerned with learning about computing.

### Guiding Principles

The microcomputer is a valuable resource - for both teaching and learning. It can be used for demonstration/illustration and for experiential learning. We can find some general guidelines by extraction from the introduction to the 'Recommended Statement of 16+ National Criteria for Computer Studies' **(2).**

> The widespread use of computer and microprocessors in the home, at work and in school makes it appropriate for schools to offer pupils Computer Studies, which should be a systematic introduction to computers, what they do and how they may be used in various contexts. It is important that any examinations in

Computer Studies reflect the principal trends of current computer usage and are not unduly influenced by outdated hardware and applications. Overall, greater importance should be given to the use of the computer as an information processing device and the ability to use a computer sensibly, rather than to its internal workings.

Computer Studies is concerned with pupils learning and applying the principles and skills of problem-solving in a computing context. These principles concern the analysis of a problem and the design, implementation, testing and documentation of a solution to that problem. The pupil learns these principles by studying computer applications in a wide variety of situations in the commercial, business and industrial world. The pupil should then acquire the skills by applying these principles to real situations with which they are familiar, particularly those found in a school context.

All 16+ Computer Studies syllabuses must give both a balanced education for those who end their studies of the subject at 16 and a basis for further studies in the subject or related areas. It is important that those pupils who include 16+ Computer Studies examinations as the termination of their studies receive a realistic view of the power and limitations of the computer to perform tasks which would otherwise be unduly tedious or difficult. These pupils should have practical experience of using computers, for example to write software and run packages.

Information processing should be taken to cover the representation of information by structured data, the processing of data by a computer, and the interpretation of the output to provide useful information. Information processing, therefore, subsumes aspects of data processing, process control and control technology. The term computer should be taken to cover mainframe, mini and microcomputers as well as computer based systems and devices. Microprocessors should be considered as the processing element of an information processing system.

Naturally some of these points refer specifically to courses for which there is some form of assessment. However, ideas such as 'learning principles by studying applications' are applicable to all levels of learning about computers.

**63**

## Applications

The presence of microcomputers within our schools allows pupils and teachers alike to become actively involved in the learning process. Not only can applications be discussed, they may also be investigated. Such investigations may require software that either simulates aspects of the application or is somewhat simplified.

Pupils are more likely to acquire skills and understanding if they can experience real situations with which they are familiar. There is greater potential for active pupil involvement within the learning situation, motivation is likely to improve and pupils can concentrate on the new areas of learning. This approach has been utilised in some text books. The problem is that the teacher (or teachers in different schools) is left to produce a suitable piece of software to support the study of an application. More recently, we have seen the emergence of case studies comprising pupil book, teacher book and software. One example is a Newsagent's Customer System (3). The link between the microcomputer and pupils' experiences is clearly identified in its introduction:

> Microcomputers are being used increasingly for a wide range of tasks and are also becoming commonplace in our schools. This package brings together two areas where students are already likely to have some background knowledge - using a microcomputer and the work of a newsagent. A number of students will either have delivered newspapers or know somebody who does deliver them and will thus be able to contribute materials and information themselves. However, rather than deal with the complexities of how a micro-computer can be used to determine the delivery rounds a simplified system to handle payments and provide limited customer information is considered. The possibility of producing delivery rounds is set as a task to both involve pupils and extend their thinking beyond the system considered. Thus the package may be used across the ability range.

When one covers applications described in a textbook the systems appear, generally, to function correctly and to take account of errors that might occur. The author then asks pupils to suggest what could go wrong - often requesting an example. Why not let pupils try using the 'system' to discover, for themselves, the existence of any errors? Once again, it is the Newsagent's Customer System where we find such an approach:

> Two programs, for payments and file maintenance, are provided but they have been deliberately written to allow the pupils to investigate the possible existence of errors. They will run successfully if valid data

is entered.   Some invalid data will be rejected but some will not.   Students are encouraged to try to beat the system, to criticise it and to suggest how faults may be corrected.   The aim of the package is to provide students with a clear understanding of some of the important principles of data processing and allow them to reinforce their understanding through practical experience.

We are also seeing the emergence of a vast amount of software (much of it of dubious quality) for use in a variety of curriculum areas.   For the teacher and pupil concerned with learning about computing, such development is a source of applications packages. For example, the use of a Computer Aided Design (CAD) package, albeit very simple, can be used to illustrate the graphics capability of computers.
There are three applications areas which are essential to any course about computers;   information storage/retrieval,   word processing and control technology/process control.   Much has been written about the 'information explosion'.   What is certain is that we must develop, in our pupils, the necessary information handling skills to enable them to obtain, manipulate and use information which will be available via electronic systems.   Pupil use of information handling packages can facilitate the development, and re-inforce, some of the skills required by all pupils - as well as serving as a vehicle for learning about computers.   Quite obviously, the possibility of establishing cross-curricular links exists in relation to the subject content of the 'information handling packages'.
Resource material for control applications as part of computing is slowly beginning to emerge - particularly as a result of initiatives from a few LEA's and MEP.   There is an overlap between the areas of computing   and   electronics/control   technology.   Some of the resources produced for teaching electronics can be used. The development of the BBC Buggy and associated software has obvious relevance for a study of computing.

## Data Processing

The stages involved in a data processing system may be summarised in outline as shown in figure 2:

| | | |
|---|---|---|
| | Collection: | of data required |
| | Preparation: | getting data into a usable form |
| | Input: | receiving data to be used |
| Control | Validation: | checking data is 'sensible' |
| | Processing: | carrying out operations on data |
| | Storage: | saving/amending data and records |
| | Output: | presentation of information |

**Figure 2:  Stages Involved in Data Processing**

Any data processing system consists of various interdependent parts. The larger and more complex the system, the more parts and functions are involved. This is true of manual, manual plus mechanised and computerised systems.

It is essential that pupils are aware of the principles of data processing and that they do not associate data processing purely with computers. The importance of people and human factors in a system should be stressed. Start by considering a school-based manual system, such as the 'tuck shop'. Involve pupils in actually carrying out as many of the stages in the system as possible - even if it requires a little simplification. This allows pupils to concentrate on the data processing principles within a familiar context. Move to a study of computerised system, again based on a familiar topic. Ideally you should use a computerised system for the same application considered as a manual system. This would allow pupils to concentrate on the computing aspects of an already familiar application through which they have experienced and understood the principles and techniques of data processing.

Another approach which actively involves pupils is for them to divide into groups and carry out a survey. Examples of surveys are *staff cars, television viewing habits* and *pop music tastes*. Pupils will be involved in all stages of data processing with the advantage that additional principles and techniques, such as form design, record layout, determination of validation requirements, programming and the work of computer personnel, may be incorporated as appropriate in relation to the needs and abilities of pupils. The software used may be a standard package or could be designed and produced by some of the (more able) pupils. Working with pupils can prove extremely rewarding for teachers. However, the teacher must ensure that pupils do not attempt something which is beyond either their own capabilities or that of the software package being used.

Providing suitable software exists, an interesting approach is to allow pupils to create and manipulate their own file of data. If they choose their own subjects on which to create a file, their motivation for working with it is likely to be reasonably high. At its simplest it requires data entry and retrieval. Beyond that pupils can be involved in record layout, file update and writing their own validation routines.

Applications packages can serve as a vehicle for the study of both a system and/or specific principles/techniques involved in data processing. Use of pre-prepared software can facilitate the use of more realistic examples which are likely to be beyond pupil preparation in terms of ability and time constraints.

**Programming**

If ever there was a contentious issue, that warrants a text in its own right, it is the form in which programming should exist within a course of study about computing. Early courses included requirements to study both a high-level language and a low-level language. In practice the latter was often a simulated language for which there was no clearly defined machine. As a result the links between hardware, software and data representation/manipulation were difficult to forge. The importance placed upon low-level languages has now decreased to the extent that, within schools, we generally find it only in Advanced Level courses.

Within the UK during the past 2 to 3 years, there has been a debate concerning the virtues of structured languages, such as PASCAL and COMAL, compared to those of BASIC; some people will argue that BASIC has few virtues! We have seen the emergence of structured BASIC. Another debate, slowly beginning to surface, concerns the suitability of flow diagrams as a method of expressing the solution to a problem.

Before considering the possible use of any programming language available on the schools' microcomputers, it is essential to identify your aims and determine the objectives for your pupils. A language suitable for a teacher may well not be appropriate for pupil use. In general terms the facilities available within a language, together with its structure, syntax and semantics, must reflect both the capability of those who will be using it and the objectives underlying its use. In other words, choose the right tool for the job.

Languages such as LOGO and PROLOG offer new possibilities, certainly in terms of computer literacy. Thoren (4) expresses it thus:

> Given a programming language in which words can be handled easily, one could model the character of a person by his or her speech. One could thus create conversations between Mr. Happy and Mr. Grumpy or even Emma and Mr. Woodhouse. On the other hand, given good graphics capabilities, it could be possible to model on the computer display the tropisms of insects like wood lice and of small rodents like rats and mice.

Whilst Thorne rightly stresses that we have yet to discover whether either PROLOG or LOGO is learnable under prevailing classroom conditions, it may well be that such languages will meet your aims and objectives. For example, do you need a live computer programming language to enable pupils to understand the concept of a program as a set of instructions?

Until recently, pupils' practical programming experience revolved around fairly simple numerical problems. However, over 90% of computing is commercial computing, involving relatively little numerical work. Yet even now we see this link between computing and mathematics dominating some new developments. Thorne illustrates this with reference to LOGO.

**67**

Too many people are publishing collections of Turtle Graphics routines with a drill and practice text book and calling the result LOGO. As a result, to many teachers LOGO means drawing pictures on the screen. They're not quite sure why this is a good thing except possibly for mathematics because it is obvious that geometry is involved.

But what makes LOGO so good for modelling is not just the Turtle Graphics. Rather it is the surroundings in which these particular facilities are embedded: the ability to solve a big problem by breaking it down into totally independent subproblems which when solved and combined polish off the whole; the ability to manipulate text easily and to process lists of information; the ability to do recursive programming. Without these features, use of LOGO outside of mathematics is virtually impossible whilst the possibilities within mathematics are but a shadow of those available from real LOGO.

We must consciously move away from a pre-occupation with numeric problems. Our microcomputers have graphics, text handling and sound capabilities - why not use them? Let me outline two problems which might be given to pupils learning a computer programming language (I will assume BASIC) for the first time.

**Problem 1:** Input a temperature in degrees Fahrenheit, convert it to Centigrade and output this new temperature. The formula to convert from Fahrenheit to Centigrade is:

$$\text{Centigrade Temperature} = (\text{Fahrenheit Temperature} - 32 \times \frac{5}{9}$$

**Sample Outputs:**

Fahrenheit temperature ? 60    Fahrenheit temperature ? 90
Centigrade temperature is 16.6  Centigrade temperature is 32.2

1(a)                              2(b)

**Problem 2:**

Draw a diamond shape on the screen of the microcomputer

**Sample Outputs:**

2(a)                         2(b)

Firstly, I would suggest that Problem 2 and its solution are more interesting/motivating than Problem 1. Now, for both problems, one of the sample outputs is incorrect. Quite obviously pupils can identify their own mistakes (surely an essential objective) far more readily from the graphic output. The program that produces the diamond shape lends itself more readily to valid amendment and thus can serve as a vehicle for the concepts and techniques associated with program editing and storage. At a more advanced level, pupils can manipulate text or combine sound and graphics.

I would like to see teachers using an individualised learning and activity approach for the study of programming. All too often 'the class' is given a programming problem. The class will contain pupils with a wide range of problem solving, communication and progamming skills that are all meant to find expression by tackling and solving a single problem. I like to see pupils building up a profile that reflects their knowledge, understanding, skills and development. Practically, this requires pupils to produce a 'programming folder' containing their work. After the introduction of new material there should be a range of programming problems for pupils to tackle. These problems would differ in terms of topic, methods of solution, expression of solution, coding requirements, testing requirements, expansion capability, adaptability, etc. In this way pupils can fulfill their potential in an area of study that motivates most of them and yet can prove to be an uncanny discriminator.

Finally, let me return briefly to the debates concerning 'BASIC, or not BASIC ...' and 'the place of flow diagrams'. Within this paper I have deliberately avoided joining these debates. What I have done is to advocate using the right tool for the job. However, we can not teach our pupils a variety of programming languages. Our choice is often constrained by such things as hardware capabilities/capacity and software implementations. Decisions should be based upon the educational objectives that have been determined. Bear in mind that programming encompasses a variety of communication skills that are demanding, of pupil and teacher alike. For example, if the visual impact of a loop in a flow diagram is the most appropriate means of communicating with a particular group of pupils then use it. If you want to use a programming language to support other areas within a study of computing, then ensure that the expression of what is to be carried out will not obscure the principles/techniques/skills you wish pupils to acquire.

**Communications and Information Technology**

Quite obviously this area could be completely subsumed within *applications.* I have already highlighted the importance of providing pupils with information handling skills. The need to include the use of information retrieval and word processing software has previously been stressed.

The concept of linking devices for data transmission is essential if pupils are to understand the functions available on communications systems and to appreciate both their current and potential significance. With this understanding, and some practical experience, pupils will become sufficiently confident to handle the range of public and private access and interactive systems they will undoubtedly meet as we move towards the 21st century.

Pupils should experience use of Teletext and Viewdata systems and be able to compare them. PRESTEL is an obvious choice but remember that having pulled down pages from PRESTEL, it is possible to manipulate those pages locally within schools. Software, for some of the more popular microcomputers within education, is now available and can provide not only a local viewdata system but facilities for actually creating pages and adding them to your own database.

Networks allow computing resources to be shared and requests for processing to be routed to the most appropriate location for processing. The actual transmission of data can take place without the recipient, or even the author, being aware of it. Networking facilities are likely to become more prevalent in our schools. In that case pupils can be actively involved, using a network, in a variety of ways. There is software to enable microcomputers to link into commercially available electronic mail systems. Once again pupils should have experience of using an electronic mail system which is one possible use of a network. Pupils may already be familiar with using a communication system. For example, either discussing or using a cash point terminal outside a bank could provide the basis upon which communications may be introduced. This would afford the opportunity to work from practical experience back towards concepts and principles.

**Implications**

Enabling pupils to develop an understanding of the social and economic effects arising from the use of computerised systems, is likely to be the most difficult task confronting the teacher of computing. Pupils lack experience in the world of work and commerce, etc. There is no easy way to achieve the levels of understanding we would like to see within our pupils. If there is a guiding principle it is that we should work out from a familiar context.

Rather than introducing *implications* as a topic, one should lead naturally into their consideration from the study of an application.

For example, studying the variety of uses that banks make of computers can lead to considerations of the accuracy of data and into discussion related to privacy and access to confidential data. Whilst the teacher must obviously have determined learning objectives and will have a learning structure in mind, one must always remain flexible in picking up and developing points and views expressed by pupils.

Pupils often lack the ability to clearly express their views - particularly using the written word. Thus the use of examples, both globally (as with an application) and locally (possibly school-based) can provide a focal point for discussion and expression. I have found that small discussion groups lead to greater individual participation.

A case study approach can prove most productive. Pupils are provided with background material. This can be in the form of documents, newspaper articles, pictures, audio tapes, tape-slide presentations, video tapes, films, visiting speakers, etc. Situations are then identified and pupils asked to discuss and respond to them. In this way pupils' experience an empathy that facilitates the understanding of effects associated with, and arising from, the use of computerised systems. There is no reason why the situations that are utilised have to be totally realistic. Here is an ideal opportunity to ask questions of the type: "What if ....". It is essential to draw together common themes, problems, effects, etc. as well as identifying and correcting misconceptions. Where appropriate draw parallels with manual systems, posing questions such as: "Is a document safer in a filing cabinet or held on a disc?".

A thematic approach may be adopted. For example, the possibility and effect of a 'cashless society' may be used to draw together a number of areas directly affecting and relating to implications. Above all, pupils must be stimulated (provoked if necessary) into *thinking* about computerised systems, their effects, possible solutions or actions.

### Hardware

All too often hardware is seen as an entity in itself rather than in the context of its use. The Working Party of the British Computer Society Schools Committee (5) expressed the need thus:

> It is not necessary to emphasise a study of hardware for its own sake, because technology changes and what is available today may well be out of date in five years time. However, as pupils are made aware of particular applications of the computer by means of case studies, it will be natural to consider the role played by particular pieces of hardware, to appreciate the facilities offered by them and to consider the relative merits (and disadvantages) of alternative devices. Pupils should view hardware as tools which are intended to be convenient for the job being undertaken.

The use of a CAD package could form the basis for the study of joysticks and lead to a consideration of light pen and graphics tablet. Ideally these devices should be available, with appropriate software, for pupils to use. Disc storage could be introduced and considered via the study of an application that required it. Production of duplicate copies of files, programs, discs or tapes could well form the basis for an integrated study of hardware, software and file management aspects of security/archiving.

One inherent danger in using the microcomputer as the vehicle for practical experience, is that pupils may confuse what happens in the 'world beyond school' with their experiences in the classroom. When using a simplified/simulated system then this fact must be stressed. Visits to local companies and visiting speakers are useful methods for broadening pupils learning experiences. However, if possible pupils should experience the use of computer systems other than microcomputers. They should be aware of the range of general purpose and special purpose computers that exist.

Audio-visual resources, in particular some of the video cassettes now becoming available, are invaluable for the study of hardware or, at a lower level, illustrating a device in operation.

## Summary

Teaching about computing is a demanding task which can prove extremely rewarding. Teachers must try to keep abreast of current applications and developments. Links should be established with local industry both for professional development/enhancement and as a source for visits and information. I have not attempted to be, in any way, prescriptive but rather to be imaginative and realistic in suggesting possible approaches to teaching about computing. Resources vary both within and between Local Education Authorities. However, each approach has developed as a result of many interconnected experiences and has been found to be successful *in the classroom*. Hopefully, we shall soon begin to see teachers from a wide variety of disciplines teaching about computing. Above all, people who teach about computing must be imaginative, visionary, flexible and responsive to the ever changing field both within and about which they provide education.

## REFERENCES

1. ICL Computer Education in Schools Newsletter, Number 40 (December 1982).

2. Recommended Statement of 16+ National Criteria for Computer Studies, G.C.E. and C.S.E. Boards' Joint Council for 16+ National Criteria (1982).

3. Weston, P.R., Newsagents Customer System: a data processing case study, ICL Computer Education in Schools, Reading (1982).

4.    Thorne, M., Modelling Work, Times Educational Supplement (27th May, 1983).

5.    Syllabuses for the Future Schools Committee Working Party, British Computer Society (1980).

# A BEGINNER'S GUIDE TO LOGO

Harold Abelson

In the 1960's, computers were very expensive and did not have much memory. Since programs had to use memory sparingly, computer languages were designed to reflect this concern. Languages had to be simple for the computer, even at the expense of being cumbersome for the programmer.

The languages of the 1960's flourished with the personal computers of the 1970's, which, although no longer very expensive, still did not have much memory. As personal computers became more popular people began to confuse the idea that a language that is simple for a computer would also be simple for people. Some people even rationalized that the cumbersome features of such languages were actually advantageous. ("If it's too easy to edit programs, you won't write them carefully in the first place.") And when educators explored the potential uses of computers, they often accepted the drawbacks of these languages as an integral part of programming.

Over the past 10 years, a different approach to educational computing has been taken. Rather than accept the limitations of affordable computers (by the standards of those days), we worked with the largest research computers available. The system we used, called Logo, is essentially a dialect of LISP, a powerful language developed for research in artificial intelligence, and used a great deal of memory compared to standards of the 1960's.

In working with Logo, we have discovered some important things. A computer language can be both simple and powerful at the same time. In fact, these two aspects are complementary rather than conflicting because it is the very lack of expressive power in primitive languages such as BASIC that makes it difficult for beginners to write simple programs that do interesting things. More important, we have found that it is possible to give people control over powerful computational resources, which they can use as tools in learning and exploring. This has often required us to go beyond ordinary considerations of computer-language design to create compelling images of how computation can provide a perspective for reformulating traditional ideas from science and mathematics to make them more accessible, more in tune with intuitive modes of thought. Working with preschool, elementary, junior high, high school, college students, we have used Logo to introduce

**75**

programming and the computational perspective at all levels. This chapter demonstrates what it is like to program using Logo, a simple but powerful system, enabling one to explore with a computer.

### Drawing with the Turtle

We begin with a look at turtle graphics. The turtle is a small triangular pointer on the screen that responds to a few simple commands. **FORWARD** moves the turtle in the direction it is facing a given number of units. If you type the Logo command **FORWARD 50**, the turtle will respond by moving forward 50 turtle steps (about ¼ the height of the screen). **RIGHT** rotates the turtle clockwise a given number of degrees. **BACK** and **LEFT** cause the movements opposite to **FORWARD** and **RIGHT**. The turtle also carries a pen, which leaves a trace of its path on the screen as it moves while the pen is down. The commands **PENUP** and **PENDOWN** make the turtle raise and lower the pen. Figure I shows the result of a simple sequence of Logo commands.

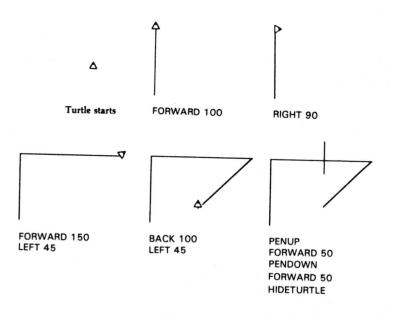

Turtle starts  FORWARD 100  RIGHT 90

FORWARD 150
LEFT 45

BACK 100
LEFT 45

PENUP
FORWARD 50
PENDOWN
FORWARD 50
HIDETURTLE

**Figure I: Moving the turtle with a simple sequence of Logo commands**

It is interesting to make drawings by using these commands (together with a few others, such as **CLEARSCREEN**, which erases the screen), but in order to really make progress, you have to teach the computer some new words. For instance, you can teach the computer that the turtle can draw a square by repeating this sequence four times: go FORWARD 50 steps, turn RIGHT 90 degrees. The Logo commands would be:

**TO SQUARE**
**REPEAT 4  (FORWARD 50 RIGHT 50)**
**END**

SQUARE is an example of Logo procedure. The first line (signalled by TO) specifies the name of the procedure. This procedure happens to be called SQUARE (since that is what it draws), but you could have called it anything. The rest of the procedure (the procedure's body) specifies the list of instructions to be carried out in response to the command SQUARE; the word END indicates the end of the definition.

Once defined in this way, SQUARE becomes part of the computer's vocabulary. Whenever you give the command SQUARE, the turtle will draw a square.

### Procedures with Inputs

An important difference exists between SQUARE and FORWARD. SQUARE always draws a square 50 steps on a side. But FORWARD is more versatile; it takes an input that determines how far the turtle should move. You can change the SQUARE procedure so that it also takes an input that determines the size of the square to be drawn. For example:

**TO SQUARE: SIZE**
**REPEAT 4  (FORWARD : SIZE RIGHT 90)**
**END**

You use SQUARE just as you would any Logo command that takes an input. That is, to draw a square with 100-step sides, you type:

**SQUARE 100**

To draw a square with 50-step sides, you type:

**SQUARE 50**

The definition of SQUARE illustrates the general rule for defining procedures that take inputs. You choose a name for the input and include it in the procedure title line preceded by a colon. Then you use the input name (with the colon) in the procedure body wherever you would normally use the value of the input.

Since a procedure, once defined, becomes just another word the computer "knows", you can use procedures as parts of the definitions of other procedures. Figure 2 shows a procedure that produces a design by repeatedly going forward, turning, and drawing a square.

**77**

```
TO DESIGN
REPEAT 6   (FORWARD 20 RIGHT 60 SQUARE 75)
END
```

**Figure 2: A design created by a simple Logo program**

### Simple Recursive Procedures

This next procedure also draws a square of a specified size:

```
TO SQ :SIZE
FORWARD :SIZE
RIGHT 90
SQ :SIZE
END
```

Although **SQ** and **SQUARE** both draw squares, they behave very differently. Instead of drawing a square and then stopping, **SQ** makes the turtle retrace the same path over and over, or until you tell the computer to stop. Here is why this happens. When you give the command:

**SQ 100**

the turtle must go **FORWARD 100, RIGHT 90,** and then do **SQ 100** again, and so on, and so on.

Add a second input to **SQ** and you obtain a procedure called **POLY**, which repeats over and over the sequence: go **FORWARD** some fixed distance, and turn **RIGHT** some fixed angle. The procedure takes as inputs the size of each **FORWARD** step and the amount of each turn:

```
TO POLY :SIZE :ANGLE
FORWARD :SIZE
```

```
RIGHT :ANGLE
POLY :SIZE :ANGLE
END
```

To use the **POLY** procedure, type the word **POLY,** followed by specific values for the inputs:

**POLY 60 144**

Figure 3 shows some of the many different shapes obtained by calling **POLY** with various inputs.

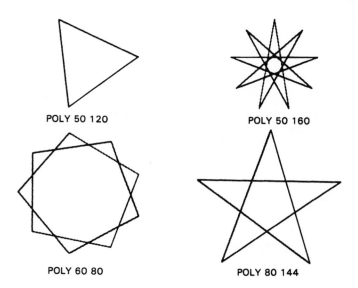

POLY 50 120          POLY 50 160

POLY 60 80          POLY 80 144

**Figure 3: Shapes drawn by the Logo program POLY**

Recursion is the programming word to describe the ability to use a procedure as part of its own definition. **SQ** and **POLY** are recursive procedures of a very simple form - they merely repeat an unchangeable cycle over and over. But recursion is a much more powerful idea and can be used to obtain much more complicated effects. To take just a small step beyond the purely repetitive kind of recursion, consider:

```
TO POLYSPI :SIZE :ANGLE
FORWARD :SIZE
RIGHT :ANGLE
POLYSPI :SIZE + 3 :ANGLE
END
```

Giving the command

**POLYSPI 1 120**

leads to this sequence of turtle moves:

```
FORWARD 1
RIGHT 120
FORWARD 4
RIGHT 120
FORWARD 7
RIGHT 120
FORWARD 10
RIGHT 120
```

which produces a triangular spiral in which each of the sides is three steps larger than the previous side. Figure 4 shows some of the shapes generated by the **POLYSPI** procedure.

Figure 4: Shapes drawn by the Logo program POLYSPI

As a variant, you can replace the **FORWARD** step in **POLYSPI** by a command that draws a square:

```
TO SPINSQUARE :SIZE :ANGLE
SQUARE :SIZE
RIGHT :ANGLE
SPINSQUARE :SIZE + 3 :ANGLE
END
```

The result of running

**SPINSQUARE 1 10**

as shown in Figure 5 is a sequence of squares of increasing size starting with a square of one-step size. Each square is three units larger than the previous one and rotated from it by 10 degrees. The procedure keeps growing until you tell Logo to stop.

**Figure 5:  Shapes drawn by SPINSQUARE - a simple recursive program**

You can also modify the procedure so that it stops when a certain size (eg 100 steps) by including a stop rule:

```
TO SPINSQUARE :SIZE :ANGLE
IF :SIZE   100 THEN STOP
SQUARE :SIZE
RIGHT :ANGLE
SPINSQUARE :SIZE + 3 :ANGLE
END
```

Part of the power of recursion is the fact that such simple programs can lead to such varied results.

## An Environment for Exploring

As you can see from the examples presented so far, it is very easy to get started in programming with turtle graphics. This is partly because of the subject matter of turtle graphics. The basic commands have simple, visible effects. At the same time, turtle graphics is an incredibly rich area for exploration in which even simple programs can have unexpected, often beautiful results. The small amount of Logo we have seen so far is enough to support weeks of activities in programming and mathematics, exploring such questions as "How does the shape of a POLY figure depend on the angle input?" or "Why do so many repeated programs produce symmetric designs?" or simply creating beautiful patterns.

In addition to the subject matter, the system interaction also plays a crucial role. When people explore using Logo, they are continually defining new procedures and modifying old ones. Much of the effort in implementing Logo has gone into providing a programming environment that makes it easy to define and modify procedures. For example the Apple implementation of Logo includes an integrated screen editor. Giving the command **TO** or **EDIT** activates the screen editor, with the appropriate procedure definition ready to be modified. A single keystroke installs the new definition as a Logo procedure.

The success of turtle geometry is due in large part to the fact that in designing it we did not view ourselves solely as mathematicians and educators attempting to invent a new approach to geometry, nor as computer scientists attempting to implement a system. Instead, we tried to take both perspectives, continually tailoring the computer system to fit the mathematics, and vice versa.

## Outputs

We have already seen how to define procedures that require inputs. You can also make a procedure output a value. For instance, the following procedure takes two numbers as inputs and outputs their average:

```
TO AVERAGE :X :Y
OUTPUT (:X + :Y)/2
END
```

The result returned by **AVERAGE** can be examined directly (using **PRINT**) or used in turn as an input for other operations:

**PRINT (AVERAGE 2 3)**
2.5
**PRINT (AVERAGE 1 2) + (AVERAGE 3 4)**
5.0
**PRINT (AVERAGE (AVERAGE 1 2) 3)**
2.25

Note the Logo convention of using parentheses to group a procedure with its inputs. Although parentheses are almost always optional in simple Logo lines, it is a good idea to include them because they make the lines easier to read.

### Programming with Procedures

A Logo program is typically structured as a cluster of procedures. These procedures pass information among themselves by means of inputs and outputs. The advantage of this kind of organisation is that it separates the program into manageable pieces, as each procedure can be simple in itself. Even in a complex program, it is unusual to have an individual procedure that is more than a few lines long. In addition, the integrated Logo editor and the general interactive nature of the Logo system enable you to define and test individual procedures separately.

   To illustrate procedural organisation, let us design a simple game that is played as follows. The computer chooses at random a "mystery point" on the screen, and asks the player to make successive LEFT and FORWARD moves with the turtle. Before each move, the computer prints the turtle's distance from the mystery point. The goal is to get the turtle very close to the point in as few moves as possible. Here is a transcript of the game in action. The computer's responses are printed in italics to distinguish them from what the player types:

*DISTANCE TO POINT IS 67.6*
*TURN LEFT HOW MUCH?*
**0**
*GO FORWARD HOW MUCH?*
**25**
*DISTANCE TO POINT IS 90.25*
*TURN LEFT HOW MUCH?*
**180**
*GO FORWARD HOW MUCH?*
**50**
*DISTANCE TO POINT IS 47.38*
.
.

*DISTANCE TO POINT IS 12.08*
*YOU WON IN 11 MOVES!*

The heart of the program is a procedure called **PLAY**. This takes as input a number M, which indicates the number of moves so far. **PLAY** first checks to see if the player has won. If so, it prints a message saying how many moves have occurred, and stops. Otherwise, it asks the player to make a move, and goes on to the next round, with **M** increased by 1:

```
TO PLAY :M
TEST CHECKWIN?
IFTRUE (PRINT (YOU WON IN):M(MOVES!))
IF TRUE STOP
MAKEMOVE
PLAY :M + I
END
```

The **PLAY** procedure is simple in itself because it delegates the problems of testing for wins and making moves to the procedures **CHECKWIN?** and **MAKEMOVE**.
Here is **MAKEMOVE**, which prompts the user for angles and distances, and moves the turtle correspondingly. It uses a subprocedure **READNUMBER**, which returns a number typed in at the keyboard.

```
TO MAKEMOVE
PRINT (TURN LEFT HOW MUCH?)
LEFT READNUMBER
PRINT (GO FORWARD HOW MUCH?)
FORWARD READNUMBER
END
```

To check for a win, the program must test whether the turtle's position is close to some predetermined point (eg 20 steps). The Logo primitive operations **XCOR** and **YCOR** return the turtle's x and y coordinates. We suppose that the x and y coordinates of the hidden point are given by variables **XPT** and **YPT**. If you assume there is a procedure **DISTANCE** that returns the distance between two points, the **CHECKWIN?** procedure can be written as follows:

```
TO CHECKWIN?
MAKE "D DISTANCE XCOR YCOR :XPT :YPT
(PRINT  (DISTANCE TO POINT IS)  :D)
IF :D  20 OUTPUT "TRUEOUTPUT" FALSE
END
```

**CHECKWIN?** returns as its value either **TRUE** or **FALSE**, which is the result that is tested by **PLAY** to determine whether the game is over. Observe also the use of the **MAKE** statement to assign values to variables. In this case, **D** is used to designate the distance.

Here is the procedure for computing the distance between two points, as the square root of the sum of the squares of the coordinates differences:

```
TO DISTANCE :A :B :X :Y
MAKE "DX :A - :X
MAKE "DY :B - :Y
OUTPUT SQRT (:DX * :DX + :DY * :DY)
END
```

Now you need a procedure to start the game:

```
TO GAME
CLEARSCREEN
MAKE "XPT RANDOMCOORD
MAKE "YPT RANDOMCOORD
PLAY 0
END
```

This clears the screen, assigns values (chosen at random) to the mystery-point coordinates **XPT** and **YPT**, and calls **PLAY** with an initial **M** equal to zero.

The following procedure, used to select random coordinates, returns a random number between -75 and +75. It works by calling the Logo primitive **RANDOM** to obtain a random number between 0 and 150, and subtracts 75 from the result:

```
TO RANDOMCOORD
OUTPUT  (RANDOM 150)  -75
END
```

The only thing needed to complete the program is READNUMBER, which returns a number input from the keyboard:

```
TO READNUMBER
OUTPUT FIRST REQUEST
END
```

READNUMBER uses the Logo primitive **REQUEST**, which waits for the user to type a line, and then returns a list of all the items in that line. The desired number is extracted as the first item of the input list (we describe lists below).

Actually, it might be better to design **READNUMBER** so that it checks to see if the item to be returned is indeed a number, and to complain otherwise:

```
TO READNUMBER
MAKE "TYPEIN FIRST REQUEST
IF NUMBER? :TYPEIN OUTPUT :TYPEIN
```

```
PRINT   (PLEASE TYPE A NUMBER)
OUTPUT READNUMBER
END
```

Notice the final line of the procedure. Its effect is to make READNUMBER try again for an input until it gets a number, as many times as necessary.

## Lists

We have seen that Logo's procedural organisation makes it an easy and convenient language for writing programs. Most modern programming languages are, in fact, procedurally organised, although few languages make it so easy to interactively define and modify procedures as does Logo.

A much more special aspect of Logo is the way it handles collections of data. This is done using lists. A list is a sequence of data objects. For example:

(1 2 BUCKLE MY SHOE)

is a list of five things. The items in a list can themselves be lists, as in:

((PETER PAN)  WENDY JOHN)

which is a list of three items, the first of which is itself a list of two items. Similarly, we can have lists whose items are lists, and so on. Lists, therefore, are a natural way to represent hierarchical structures, that is, structures composed of parts that themselves are composed of parts.

Logo includes a number of operations for manipulating lists. FIRST extracts the first item of the list. In this example:

FIRST  (1 2 BUCKLE MY SHOE)

it is 1, and in the next example:

FIRST  ((PETER PAN)  WENDY JOHN)

it is (PETER PAN)

The BUTFIRST operation returns the list consisting of all but the first item of the given list, so in

BUTFIRST  (1 2 BUCKLE MY SHOE)

it is (2 BUCKLE MY SHOE), while in

BUTFIRST  ((PETER PAN)  WENDY JOHN)

**86**

A Beginner's Guide to Logo

it is **(WENDY JOHN)**.

The **FPUT** operation takes the two objects x and y and constructs a list whose **FIRST** is x and whose **BUTFIRST** is y. For example:

**FPUT 5  (2 BUCKLE MY SHOE)**

produces the list   **(5 2 BUCKLE MY SHOE)**, and

**FPUT  (PETER PAN)**
**(BUCKLE MY SHOE)**

produces the list   **((PETER PAN) BUCKLE MY SHOE)**.

The **SENTENCE** operation, like **FPUT**, constructs larger lists from smaller ones, but in a slightly different way.  **SENTENCE** takes a number of lists as inputs and combines all their elements to produce a single list. For example:

**SENTENCE (PETER PAN)**
**(BUCKLE MY SHOE)**

produces the list   **(PETER PAN BUCKLE MY SHOE)**.

The significant thing about lists in Logo is that they can be manipulated as what computer scientists call "firstclass data objects."  That is to say, Logo lists (as opposed, for example, to arrays in BASIC) can be:

* assigned as the values of variables
* passed as inputs to procedures
* returned as the outputs of procedures

For instance, you can assign names to lists:

**MAKE "X  (OOM PAH)**
**MAKE "Y  (HEIGH HO)**

and then refer to the values of these variables, so that **BUTFIRST :X** is the list **(PAH)**. You can also combine operations on lists to produce more complex operations. For example:

**FIRST FIRST  ((PETER PAN)  WENDY JOHN)**

returns the word **PETER**.

You can also write procedures that manipulate lists:

**TO DOUBLE :L**
**OUTPUT SENTENCE :L :L**
**END**

PRINT DOUBLE (OOM PAH)
*OOM PAH OOM PAH*

PRINT DOUBLE DOUBLE (OOM PAH)
*OOM PAH OOM PAH*
*OOM PAH OOM PAH*

The implication of this is that you can combine operations on lists, much as you combine operations on numbers in ordinary languages. For example, one very useful list operation is **PICKRANDOM**, which chooses an item at random from an input list. **PICKRANDOM** is not provided as a primitive operation, but is easily constructed out of simpler operations, such as finding the length of a list, selecting a random number in a given range, and extracting the nth item of a list.

### Playing with Text

To illustrate how lists are used, let us examine a program that composes vacation postcards, such as:

```
DEAR DOROTHY            DEAR MARY
WISH YOU WERE HERE.     EVERYONE'S FINE
LOVE — JOHN             WRITE SOON — AUNT EM
```

You begin by setting up lists of names and phrases from which the elements of the postcard will be chosen:

```
MAKE      "NAMES           MAKE      "PHRASES
          (JOHN                      (WISH YOU WERE HERE.)
          DOROTHY                    (WEATHER'S GREAT!)
          (AUNT EM)                  (SURF'S UP.)
          OCCUPANT)                  (EVERYONE'S FINE.))

              MAKE      "CLOSINGS
                        (LOVE
                        (SEE YOU SOON)
                        (WRITE SOON))
```

Here is the main postcard program:

```
TO POSTCARD
PRINT SENTENCE (DEAR) NAME
PRINT BODY
PRINT (SENTENCE CLOSING (-) NAME)
POSTCARD
END
```

The recursive call in the last line makes the procedure keep printing new postcards over and over. (Compare the **SQ** and **POLY** procedures). The procedures **NAME, BODY,** and **CLOSING** generate the elements of the postcard by selecting items from the appropriate lists:

```
TO NAME                          TO BODY
OUTPUT PICKRANDOM:NAMES          OUTPUT PICKRANDOM:PHRASES
END                              END
```

```
               TO CLOSING
               OUTPUT PICKRANDOM :CLOSINGS
               END
```

You can change the postcard program so that it automatically augments its repertoire of phrases by every so often (say, one chance in three) asking the user to type in a new phrase and adding that to the **PHRASES.** To do this, we add to the **POSTCARD** procedure the line:

```
IF I.IN.3 LEARN.NEW.PHRASE
```

The **I.IN.3** procedure returns **TRUE** with odds of one chance in three and **FALSE** otherwise. One possible way to write this procedure is:

```
TO I.IN.3
IF (RANDOM 3) = 0 OUTPUT "TRUE
OUTPUT "FALSE
END
```

Here's how the program learns a new phrase:

```
TO LEARN.NEW.PHRASE
PRINT (PLEASE TYPE IN A NEW PHRASE)
MAKE "PHRASES FPUT REQUEST
    :PHRASES
END
```

The idea is that **REQUEST** returns (as a list) the phrase that the user types in response to the message. This is added to **PHRASES** (by means of **FPUT**), so that the program will be able to use this phrase in future postcards, like:

*PLEASE TYPE IN A NEW PHRASE*
DON'T FORGET TO FEED THE DOG

DEAR OCCUPANT
DON'T FORGET TO FEED THE DOG
LOVE — JOHN
.
.
.

Text-generation procedures are fun to write and to play with and also easy to modify. You can make them as elaborate or as simple as you like and apply the same ideas to producing essays, poems and so on.

## The Computational Perspective

Logo is often described as a programming language. Those of us who designed Logo tend to think of it rather as a computer-based learning environment, where the activities (exploring the symmetry of POLY) are just as integral as the programming tools used (recursion and lists). Logo is also a continually evolving environment, and the microcomputer implementations of Logo that have appeared during the past year are only the first to be widely available. We plan to extend Logo to incorporate new linguistic features as well as new activities, such as a computer-based physics curriculum that builds upon turtle geometry. At the MIT Laboratory for Computer Science, the Educational Computing Group is designing a follow-on system to Logo suitable for the new generation of personal computers that will be coming into use during the latter half of the 1980s.

The next few years will be exciting ones in educational computing because personal computers are becoming powerful enough to support systems that are designed for the convenience of people rather than for the convenience of compilers. If we can dispel the delusion that learning about computers should be an activity of fiddling with array indexes and worrying about whether X is an integer or a real number, we can begin to focus on programming as a source of ideas. For programming is an activity of describing things. The descriptions are phrased so that they can be interpreted by a computer, but that is not really so important. Computational descriptions, like those of science or mathematics, provide a perspective, a collection of "tools of thought", such as procedural organisation, hierarchical structure, and recursive formulations. Logo, and languages like it, will help make these tools available to everyone.

# THE ITMA COLLABORATION - HISTORY, TASKS, - SOME ANSWERS TO QUESTIONS

Rosemary Fraser

Since 1978, Investigations on Teaching with Microcomputers as an Aid (ITMA) has been growing and changing the tasks that it set itself. This chapter describes the current state, how the Collaboration is presently organised, and its approach and methodology to exploring the potential of the computer in the classroom. ITMA grew out of an early recognition that, while the mainstream of CAL was still concerned with the individual students' learning with a computer, the potential as a *teaching* aid in the classroom was a rich and complex area that merited systematic attention. Various factors made this a timely contribution - the class based organisation of schools, the level of hardware provision, and the efforts of other teachers who had been trying things along similar lines in their own classrooms all gave this work central relevance.

The ITMA approach is centrally based on classroom observation of programs in use, and thus on the work of the many teacher-developers in various subjects who have worked with our draft material. This empirical approach is central both to increasing our understanding of the effects of the microcomputer in the classroom and to the development of teaching material in the form of program teaching units. Various people at other centres have contributed importantly to the programme of work - with strategic advice, with specific ideas, or with work on their development. The devising of new, more cost effective, techniques for recording what happens in the classroom has been an important factor in the work of the Collaboration (1). The other facet which must be emphasised is that of teacher training - most curriculum innovations fail to make any large scale impact because the problems in helping teachers to absorb and adapt to them are under-estimated; ITMA has done some new things in this area too.

During 1982, the various aspects of ITMA's work became even more closely linked. The early findings of the MMET Research Study (Micros and Mathematics Extended Trial) (2) guided the in-service training material prepared under the title Micros and Mathematics Classroom (MMC) (3) for which a special introductory pack of program teaching units was assembled, developed and published under the same title (4). This integration of classroom studies, program developments and teacher training is a characteristic feature of ITMA's approach.

All this work was a joint effort of the Nottingham and Plymouth groups, also involving others elsewhere. The same is true of the current work on the primary curriculum and in other areas. Five specific areas of general responsibility have been established - administration, curriculum and research, classroom studies, program teaching units, development and training. The aim was not to make any substantial changes to the way ITMA operated but to forward the multitude of tasks that the Collaboration has in hand. The diagrams shown in Figure 1 give a summary view of these tasks. In each case, the central column summarizes the main activities in the area while the rectangular boxes show the principle outputs from the work involved. The inter-dependance of the three areas of activities is illustrated in the way that the outputs from one area figure prominently among the inputs into others, shown as 'clouds' on the diagram system.

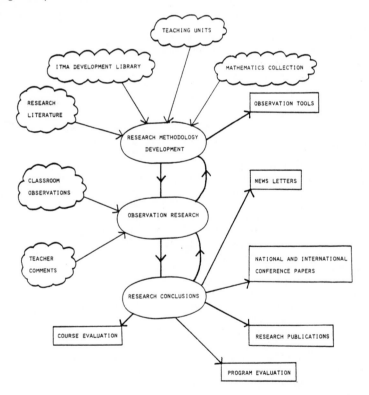

**Figure 1(a): Classroom Studies**

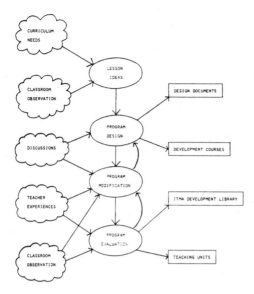

**Figure l(b): Program development**

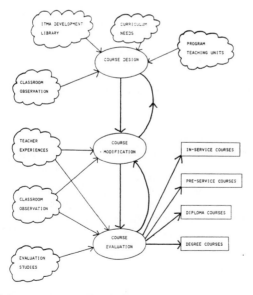

**Figure l(c): Teacher training**

We conclude this introduction with a sequence of question and answers which aim to show in non-technical terms something of the essence of the ITMA approach.

*Why should we bother?*

Teachers are busy people - are there good reasons to distort their established ways of working by encouraging them to use the micro? We think it is at least worth investigating how far the gains are worth the effort, and early results have shown promise. The computer is a powerful and versatile tool which has helped in many areas. There is plenty of room for improving the effectiveness of education. Also, the computer in the classroom provides a natural way for children to learn of its strength and limitations.

*What should we try to do?*

We should aim to design material that will make a *qualitative* difference to teaching and learning, showing possibilities that carry beyond a direct use of the program in suggesting further learning activities of value; in this way the inevitably small amount of good material available in the short term may have a significant and useful effect.

*What are the problems?*

Most curriculum innovation has no impact on the mainstream of teachers beyond the small group of enthusiasts who promote it. Successful exceptions have combined the imagination to offer teachers something worth the effort of changing their habits with the realism to make sure that it really works for the bulk of the 'target' group of teachers, and of pupils. In a new field with no reliable established 'craft skills', this requires a research based approach.

*What do you need to do it?*

The relative skills involved in using a new medium to serve effectively a complex set of aims, teaching styles and approaches are indeed wide. The design of images to be used to stimulate valuable learning activities is a new profession - akin to directing educational television programmes in some ways - and these professional skills will take time to develop and disseminate. You would not expect a good teacher who is simply given technical support to produce good educational television - or a good pilot to design an aeroplane; a wider range of skills is needed.

*How is ITMA doing it?*

By bringing together people of exceptional ability and a wide range of skills - teachers, subject specialists, psychologists, curriculum designers, evaluators, computer experts, programmers, graphic designers and publishers - and making sure that they see directly and in detail the effects of material of various kinds in the classrooms of ordinary teachers or various styles and approaches - and by carrying this knowledge through to helping teachers to learn to use this new medium. From all this, general lessons on design and development gradually emerge.

*What have we learnt so far?*

The micro is a versatile 'teaching assistant' whose range of roles we are only beginning to explore - blackboard, textbook, calculator, filing system, manager, questionner, explainer, unknown system to explore. While many of the programs we see merely promote drab, thought-free drill of which we already have too much in the curriculum, it is now clear that programs can be designed and developed to stimulate and support valuable learning activities of a kind that most teachers find it difficult to sustain - problem solving, discussion, theoretical and practical investigation in every subject. In very simple terms, the computer helps by temporarily taking over some of the roles which the teacher normally has to play in a natural way, that release the teacher for other more precious activities. For the near future, this 'in-service training' role may be the most important single use of the micromputer in teaching.

**The ITMA Approach**

Members of any curriculum development team producing new teaching materials need to think in fundamental ways about the knowledge, skills and concepts that the material will help to develop. They need to consider the way that people think and learn. This is particularly true when either the material or the style of learning involved is essentially new. Microcomputers, and the roles that they can play in the home and school environments, provide a surprising and powerful focus to such fundamental study. How can the exploration begin? Imagination must be a prospectus of exciting ideas to visit and explore, but it may be an unreliable guide. Experiment is the essential ingredient in discovering the effect and effectiveness of what is devised and desseminated, before loosing it on the world.

*What has emerged so far?*

The Collaboration's study so far suggest a range of possible roles for the micro in the classroom.

blackboard
textbook
teaching assistant

manager
teacher
examiner
partner
apparatus or environment
pupil

In each role the range of interactions with pupils and teachers is wide and varied. The ITMA studies so far are preliminary explorations - no doubt much more remains to emerge. What may survive in a gradually developing form is the ITMA approach - the methodology of exploration. The essential elements of this approach are theory and experiment and the way they support each other. The laboratories for the latter are the classrooms for teachers with a wide variety of styles and approaches who work with the project. The phenomena are those of learning and teaching. The instruments are materials and trained, open minded, close detailed observation. The theory, which as always guides the experimental design, is initially speculative and so, as in any new field, creative divergent thinking is needed. People from a variety of backgrounds and interests who can communicate well enough need to share their perceptions, and to develop and refine the theoretical ideas in the light of the experimental findings. The environment of the study must draw the best out of all of these. This involves developing skills:

- in communicating with each other
- in communicating with all the groups that are closely involved   and finally,
- in communicating to groups interested in understanding and sharing in the results of the study.

ITMA will always depend a great deal on the help, ideas, encouragement and support of many gifted individuals and of other practising groups in a variety of fields and disciplines. The creation of opportunities of such groups and individuals to meet and share their skills is a major organisational challenge for such a project.

The project environment needs to be managed so that the balance of activities produces the richest outcome in understanding. In each case the conversations before, between and after the sessions of the meeting are likely to be as valuable in advancing our basic understanding as the discussion within the meetings themselves. Figure 2 presents an image of the ITMA Collaboration as it is, and shows its potential for growth and development as a well founded study centre.

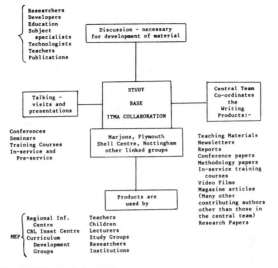

**Figure 2: The ITMA Collaboration**

The aim of the project is to establish these research and development activities in parallel with the in-service and information services within a regional, national, and an international frame. The richness of an environment that is able to link people engaged in all three facets should help to provide the cultural variety necessary for our ideas, and our understanding of learning to grow and to be tested at their point of growth.

## The Spectrum of Talents - the Need for a Change of Attitude

The established structure of professions and institutions separates scientist from educator, technologist from humanist, teacher from designer - not to mention adult from child. It can be argued that progress of basic problems, in a new field like this, demands not only that all are willing to work together, but also that an overlapping of skills is required. In a very practical sense, the ability of people to communicate is strongly dependant on their mutual understanding of each other's expertise. At present the professionals are:

*Researchers in Subject Domains* concerned with 'doing the subject' developing its content, and understanding its concepts in their own way.

*Educators,* including teachers and teacher trainers and advisers, concerned with teaching the content and concepts of the subject (and hopefully its links to other disciplines and the world outside) and thus with seeking to understand learning processes. They operate under quite heavy constraints imposed by the educational and social system

**97**

- curriculum domination by examinations for example.

*Research Psychologists* studying at a fundamental level learning processes, attitudes and behaviour guided by theoretical constructs ranging from Piaget to artificial intelligence models.

*Computer Scientists and Professional Programmers*, expert in the latest technology – and often dismayed at the quality of computing power currently available in the school educational market.

*Graphic Designers and Creative Artists* skilled in producing images and sounds and knowing how people are likely to respond to them.

At present, no professional identification exists for people who coordinate all the contributions to the design of effective teaching material. The analogy with the educational television producer, who must harness the ideas and efforts of the academic, the writer, the musician, the designer and the engineering team in producing a coherent and effective programme, maybe a useful one. A possible title for these coordinators might be *Curriculum Designers*. It is they who carry overall responsibility for the creation and production of the new curriculum materials.

As in any new profession, they now emerge from a variety of backgrounds, producing work of a great range of quality. Many operate purely instinctively; as in other professions, instinctive overall judgement will remain of paramount importance, but those who learn to work in a reasonable systematic way, taking into account a whole range of skills required, are likely develop further and faster. They are also more likely to acquire the *range* of knowledge that gives an insight into the complex problems involved in creating materials and environments that enable people to learn naturally and effectively. In its related but quite different way the development of computer science itself, from its early machine-code-mechanism to its present state as a powerful problem solving science provides another vivid example of the development of a new profession.

The Collaboration has been fortunate, through the support of various agencies and its host institutions, in being able to bring together the whole range of disciplines referred to above. It is important for the development of good educational software that more institutions and agencies encourage and foster such collaborations between people with skills in all these areas.

### Some Examples of the Collaborations Work

Micros and Mathematics Extended Trial (MMET)
Computer Aided Teaching (5) – 1983 Abstract

In order to examine some of the problems and benefits of using a microcomputer as a classroom teaching aid, we observed 174 school lessons during which 17 teachers employed a microcomputer regularly with a chosen class for a whole term. It is argued that the ergonomic factors here differ considerably from those in other man/machine interactions. Problems of screen visibility were frequently noted and the inexperience of pupil and teacher operators caused a number of difficulties. Styles of computer use were very varied and these are discussed. Although educational performance was not measured by means of test scores, the range and quality of pupil activities suggests that the educational benefits are considerable. Recommendations are made to teachers, education authorities, software designers and hardware manufacturers.

Learning Activities and Classroom Roles (6) - 1983 Abstract

This paper is concerned with the range and balance of learning activities in the classroom and with elucidating how the various roles assumed by those involved relate to these activities. The analysis is based on records of the detailed observation of 174 mathematics lessons; the use of the microcomputer as a teaching aid in parts of these lessons was a crucial element of the analysis, giving insight through its perturbation of the familiar pattern of roles and activities. This enables us to develop a taxonomy relating observable classroom activities, inferred learning activities and the roles played by the teacher, the pupils and, when it was in use, the computer. Exemplar lessons are described; they have been chosen to illustrate the taxonomy and the shifting and sharing of roles that we most commonly observed. Among other results, it is shown that the micro is regarded by the pupils as an independent 'personality' and that, suitably programmed, it can temporarily take over some of the roles usually assumed by the teacher in such a way that the teacher adopts other roles, rarely found in the classroom, that are essential to the promotion of high level learning activities.

**Implications for the Design of Program Teaching Units**

From this study, and bearing in mind related work, a number of fundamental implications emerge for the design and development of program teaching units. Some are related to ergonomic considerations others to the analysis we have presented here amplified by the detailed study of particular programs in a further research paper and of classroom interactions. We shall state them fairly baldly since the justification of general statements comes from the generality of our data rather than from particular instances, useful though these may be for illustration.

(1) *Pupil activity centering* - the designer should set his attention on the pupil learning activities that he wishes to promote, and not on the micro and its screen images which have the secondary role of stimuli for these activities. This almost self-

evident but widely ignored principle has a less obvious corollary, namely:

(2)    *Omission design* - the most important aspects should be actively produced by the pupils in their mind and on paper or some other personal medium under their direct control - so these aspects should *not* normally be shown by and on the micro.   (Even revealing them later can encourage a 'wait and see' attitude. Thus PIRATES is a program about co-ordinates that never shows a plotted point, resisting all the marvellous graphics potential of the micro.   SUBGAME never discusses strategy, while EUREKA only really 'takes fire' when you turn the cartoon off).

(3)    *Ambition* - design material that at least promises a qualitative impact in its educational benefits.   There are very few (100) program teaching units to have any effect on the whole 5-18 curriculum (50,000 hrs).   It is an effort for teachers to use them, and this situation is likely to persist - the mediocre is not worth the effort.

(4)    *Access* - the 'access level' measures the balance between ease-of-use and power; any program should be accessible to its clearly identified target audience, any extra power-plus-complexity being made available in a way that protects those without extra expertise from disagreeable experience and the dangers of dissillusionment.

(5)    *Teachers appeal* - if the teacher doesn't like it, the children won't get it.

From these a number of more specific points emerge:

(a)    *Willingness* - the program should allow the pupils and the teachers to feel that they are learning and teaching in their own way, and not in one determined by the program (so many programs officiously dominate the whole process producing a claustrophobic user reaction; only psycho-motor games have strong enough appeal safely to ignore this factor).

(b)    *Activity Centering* - since there is an enormous range and number of topics in the curriculum but relatively few important learning activities, real educational benefit is more likely to emerge if program design concentrates on promoting learning acitivtes that are valuable and elusive, such as problem solving, open investigation and discussion, rather than instructing on particular topics or providing yet more practice.

(c)    *Follow on* - look for ideas that will lead to further activities without the computer, and link to other topics and subjects.

(d)  *Recognisable usefulness* - if the teacher sees that the unit is recognisably useful in the present curriculum, particularly in awkward areas, she is likely to try it - and be led to discover its other more profound benefits.

(e)  *Showing possibilities* - a unit will be particularly worthwhile if it shows teachers new possibilities for their teaching which will carry over into other lessons, and if it supports them while they acclimatise to this new experience. This in-service training role may initially be the most important contribution of the micro.

(f)  *Supporting role shifts* - one important way of implementing (e) is through the role shifting and role sharing. The Program exemplars in this discussion should help designers to see the ingredients - clear scene-setting, solid unobtrusive task setting and management, and a task with a rich and varied strategic problem solving demand.

(g)  *Teacher-added material* - material added to the EUREKA program for example has shown how powerful the additional material can be; in this particular example the teacher produced materials point the way forward to further learning activities of value that do not require computer support.  Designers should have this aspect constantly in mind.  It may be of even greater value to design programs which allow teachers to incorporate, and to retain material in the program system itself, though the additional complexity in use should not be ignored.

We conclude this chapter with the personal comments of two educationalists on the use of microcomputers in schools.

## Stranger in Paradise (?)

Laurie Tate

By one of those odd quirks of fortune which sometimes come the way of even the most primary of headteachers I found myself in Plymouth early in January - a member of a course in 'Advanced Program Design' run by ITMA under the auspices of the CET as part of the Government's MEP (How I love all these initials......).

It was bitterly cold that first evening and 'Marjons' in no way resembled the Plymouth I remembered, perched as it was on a bleak hilltop like some white ziggurat. What am I doing here, I thought. I must be mad to leave a warm home and the peace of an office sanctum disturbed only by the patter of little feet, for *this*.

The chilliness of the climate was not diminished by the discovery that my fellow course members were all clever secondary teachers - of science, computer studies and mathematics.  What place had I, a primary head experienced only in the play way and discovery methods, with such as these?

But they all seemed pleasant enough, as did the ITMA team (with little hint of what they had in store for us). Things began to drop into perspective. The prospect of three months away from it all stretched out ahead - no travelling every day in wintry trains, no wrangles with builders over a leaky roof or frozen toilets, or unending discussions with the Social Services department, or the countless other trivialities which pass for education. Instead, the chance to play, uninterrupted, with a powerful computer, perhaps write a program or two, explore the locality... and then in the Spring, the sweet Spring, return refreshed, invigorated, ready for the summer term.

How wrong can one be? Earlier trepidation returned, became near panic, as we started in earnest. The philosophy was clear - in at the deep end, sink or swim, kill or cure. I soon knew my situation. Every day brought new relelations of the 380Z. (How I sighed for the comparative simplicity of my 'Pet'). It appeared to have been programmed to throw up every error code I had ever heard of and twice as many I had never met. And just to add salt, there were those cunningly ingenious exercises of Colin's after each session. Every day seemed to bring new knowledge, new handouts. I hadn't thought to bring a file, soon I was filling my second. We were introduced to 'Jane' - two, in fact - a bonus indeed, and 'Eureka' and 'Pirates' and 'Transpots', and 'Adventure' when Colin wasn't about.

But it was 'SCAN' that really bugged me. A scandalous idea, this. (Skandalon (GK)=obstacle, offence, stumbling block). You needed at least a gamma 3 brain as well as machine code writing speed to keep the records of observation up to the minute.

We struggled with the inevitable dilemmas of programming - speed of operation, portability, transferability, readability, structure, high and low resolution, etc., and of course, how to nobble Basic (is it nobble or knobble?) Why should anyone *want* to nobble such a beautiful language?

Suddenly, it seemed, we were half way, and our raison d'etre was brought home to us, to produce a crash proof program fit for schools in the remaining time. (How long did 'Jane' take?)

But there was the real Jane, David and Ken, ready to tear themselves away from their own studies to manage us from time to time, to keep us at boiling point, as it were, and maintain the impetus and the schedule, and there was Max, the Prof., so kind and yet so shrewd and keenly critical, now sadly missed, I imagine. So to school trials of the program, the final review, and it was over so quickly.

Posterity will judge the results of the course in terms of effective programs, but if laughter, co-operation, honest criticism, team spirit and long hours of solid work count for anything, this was success.

I am grateful a stranger from 'the Smoke' was allowed to join in.

## Mastery

Max Clowes

(Max Clowes died before this essay was completed).

### Introduction

In these notes I want to sketch an idea about one of the meanings that interacting with a computer can have. The idea is in part an attempt to re-interpret my experience over several years of the pattern(s) of interaction between undergrads and the POP I I programming system at Sussex University when following an introductory one term course in Artificial Intelligence called Computers and Thought. My attempt utilises conceptions of personal functioning called from various psycho-therapies and related 'growth' disciplines. It is also influenced - at least in relation to the role of the computer - by Seymour Papert's conception of micro-worlds.

My goal in attempting this synthesis is to provide one framework within which to carry out in-service computer training especially of teacher.

### Personal Styles

The ITMA group has drawn attention to the way in which a microcomputer used as a classroom aid can affect the structure of the interaction between teacher and pupils, and in particular can encourage, reinforce or inhibit the teacher's *personal style*. It is not easy to change one's personal style, especially in situations which demand (or may seem to) rapid response.

What can be said of the classroom can be true of life outside it too - the ways in which we habitually go about doing things is hard to recognise and hard to change, even when it doesn't seem to work. Especially in relation to others where our personal style is a seemingly vast complex of roles, goals, expectations, attitudes, judgements and beliefs that is so interconnected as to defy any alteration.

In those situations that we call academic pursuits, our personal style is perhaps synonymous with problem-solving techniques and richly infused with knowledge of the subject domain. The same is likely true of hobbies and sports and *perhaps* these styles carry a smaller superstructure of control apparatus than that which the psychotherapist has to deal with in seeking to develop the personal styles within a marriage or a family.

### Microworlds and Mastery

The procedures that constitute being a mathematician results from the mastery of experiences gained in interacting with a domain -what

Papert calls a micro-world, for example, the experiences mastered of Algebra. I suggest that we need to conceive of this microworld as one that is rich in potential experiences, experiences whose progressive assimilation leads to a sense of our being able to control or master the events of our interaction with it. We begin to make the world work for us.

The computer, Papert argues, is capable of being programmed to create microworlds which will deliver the kinds of experiences that a novice will be able to assimilate - provided that in designing that microworld we pay attention to the psycho-logic of that assimilation. Central to that psychologic is a sense of initiative, exploration, and control.

Different therapies assemble their own characteristic microworlds. 'Group' therapy seeks to create a bounded safe world within which his experiences of interaction with the group may lead a participant to a mastery of the wider social scene. For the analyst, it is himself and the setting of the consulting room which provide the microworld whose logic however dissimilar from the client's life will nevertheless evoke potentially empowering experiences for the client.

The insight of many Eastern disciplines seems to be that life itself can become just such a microworld, there is no need to create these cultural artefacts e.g. *The Tigers Cave* Leggatt. Don Juan's account of the way of the Hunter in Castereda's *Journey to Irethan* is a masterly exposition of one such discipline.

Behind all these therapies lies the conception that we, each of us is the collection of personal styles that express our mastery - however, partial - of the worlds, intellectual physical and social, with which we interact. The purpose of these disciplines is not to change these styles but by making them visible to us, confer on the pilgrim an element of our own choosing in our utilisation of them.

The problem of course lies in us - in our own inadequate perceptions of the styles we have.

## Using the Computer to Evoke a Perception of Personal Style

The Computers and Thought course had as its academic objective achieving for the student some familiarity with the computational metaphor for Human Intelligence. The vehicle for this was a computer based microworld containing a relatively small set of programs and systems with which the student was expected to interact. The interaction was largely if not wholly one involving programming - the POPII interpreter bulked very large in the students experience. So large indeed that at times it appeared that learning to program was the academic objective - a goal that the course was ill-designed to achieve.

The course became very popular, judging by the increasing numbers of students opting to follow it. What emerged however, was not always readily expressible in academic terms, rather students and faculty become concerned with the personal discussions that students seemed to make. Especially relevant to these notes are the students who become aware of 'how they went about things' - the interaction had it seems evoked an experience of personal style. The ingredients of this microworld included not only access (almost unlimited) to a powerful interactive computing system, but also enthusiastic teaching and a growing sense of membership of a rather select, if at times bewildered and embattled club. People were willing to help -to decipher error messages, to suggest design constructs, to explain obscure handouts - but for many there was never enough help. The microworld was very short on 'transitional objects' - computer based entities like Papert's TURTLE with which the novice had a prior measure of identification. This no doubt leads to the many disappointments and to some of the not inconsiderable number of drop outs.

The course was not originally designed to evoke the sort of responses that I have noted. But more and more of it began to take on that guise: often uncomfortable for students accustomed to more conventional agendas.

## Towards a Designed Environment for Evoking Personal Style

Those seemingly accidental outcomes of the course, together with the as yet ill-articulated facets of the POPII microworld that gave rise to them, do not constitute a specification for a further more planned initiative. Indeed it might be argued that no initiative is needed - these events are a likely phenomenon in any intensive residential learning environment. A number of contemporary trends argue against premature dismissal.

Rapid changes in the economic structures of the world reflected here in the U.K. in inflation, rising unemployment and a growing unease about urban violence suggest that a new measure of agency in personal style may be a vital factor in the individual's personal well-being and country's economic survival. Patterns of development for more prosperous expansionist climates no longer work in competitive recessionist chills. Among the biggest changes coming about, the computer revolution in government, businesses, industry and latterly in education threaten the established personal styles of every professional person, and sweep away the jobs of many unskilled workers. Disillusion with many aspects of contemporary school life is common amongst both pupils and staff. More than ever we depend upon a high level of technical and scientific expertise among the young, more than ever the traditional patterns of instruction which were used to accomplish that proved ineffective. Creating a greater awareness of personal style is not of course new. Management training courses, as well as personal growth movements all point to that as an established phenomenon. Harnessing the computer in the manner adumbrated by Papert and hinted at in the unplanned outcomes of the Computers and Thought course, seems

**105**

specially appropriate. For it not only utilises the labour-saving potential of the computer as a training aid, but provides a rich source of incidental learning about the very technology responsible in part for challenging existing personal styles.

While it seems likely that appropriately inventoried microworlds could be authored for evoking a perception of personal style in social and professional contexts of any kind (or so the experiences of Computers and Thought would suggest) a clearer grasp of the design characteristics would be likely to emerge from a narrow focus. In particular there is good reason to choose the classroom as a context and teachers as clients, given the contemporary drive to install microprocessors in every secondary school. It is to this task we will now turn.

## Using a Microcomputer to Illuminate the Teacher's Personal Style

Beginning studies of teacher use of classroom cpmputer programs by the ITMA project have revealed quite wide differences in the ways that teachers seek to use them. Programs (e.g. PIRATES, JANE, TRANSPOTS), designed to admit of flexible use are indeed used differently by different teachers - it seems that each teacher has a more or less fixed personal style into which new aids like an interactive computer program are adapted (or rejected). Some of the principles that govern the design of such flexible packages have been sketched out in preliminary studies by the project. These principles include the provision of simple language interface whose user semantics are topic centred, through which the user can specify the modes of behaviour of the program. These selected modes reflect the intended style of use - revision, question and answer session, group work, individual tuition, etc. Expressions in the language (for PIRATES some 100's in number) thus delimit a space of styles of use, which in principle the teacher might explore. Motivating such an exploration is of course crucial, but incentives such as a schools acquisition of a microcomputer are not insubstantial.

The setting within which such explorations might be the subject of a controlled study of computer aided evocation of personal style naturally follows. It is in in-service courses designed to train teachers in the use of these systems as classroom aids.

## REFERENCES

1.    Beeby, T., Burkhardt, H., and Fraser, R., Systematic Classroom Analysis Notation, Shell Centre, 1979.
2.    Research and Study carried out by the ITMA Collaboration, Micros and Mathematics Extended Trial (1981).
3.    Burkhardt T., and Fraser, R., Micros in the Mathematics Classroom, MEP Training Pack, 1982.
4.    ITMA Collaboration, Micros in the Mathematics Classroom, Longmans (1982)

# Using Micro-Computers in Schools

## in Schools

Edited by
Colin Terry

5.    Phillips, R., et al, Computer Aided Teaching, ITMA Publication (1983).
6.    Fraser, R., et al, Learning Activities and Classroom Roles, ITMA Publication (1983).

# A CRITICAL EXAMINATION OF THE EFFECT OF THE MICROCOMPUTER ON THE CURRICULUM

Colin Baker

## Introduction

The aim of the chapter is to provide a critical edge to discussions on the role of the microcomputer in the curriculum. It is not intended to invoke a Luddite reaction, rather to argue for greater, ongoing evaluation of expenditure at a national and school level and greater care in the use of software in the classroom.

It is probably fair to say that we live amidst a revolution and that revolution is not just technological. The Industrial Revolution of the 18th century produced a period of rapid advance, a period of unpredictable and unstoppable changes which transformed much more than just industry. It transformed the whole of man's life: wealth and health, family and social life, education and culture. In the same way, it is possible to argue that the Computer Revolution will permeate and penetrate beyond mere technological advance. It is already affecting and will further affect employment, family life, leisure time, communication. In addition, the revolution impinges on schools, education and culture. The parallel of the Computer Revolution with the Industrial Revolution heralds a warning. Change occurs so quickly that controlling that change, evaluating change in prospect rather than retrospect becomes difficult even unlikely.

### The Implications of Hardware Decisions

Under the Microelectronics Education Programme the Department of Industry and the Department of Education and Science has provided the finance to ensure that almost all primary and secondary schools obtain a microcomputer. The Government bears half the cost of specified microcomputers. Less publicized is the Government's scheme which provides teacher training establishments with a package of four different microcomputers replete with monitors and software.

Two issues arise from this policy of subsidization to schools and free samples to institutions responsible for the pre-service education of teachers. First, the assumption being made is that technological advance brought into the classroom automatically leads to educational progress. The predictions made for programmed learning and educational television in recent decades should cast doubts on the validity of that assumption. Neither media lived up to their promise. If the analogy may stand, the way microcomputers have been introduced into British classrooms is like subsidizing the introduction of physical fitness equipment into every home, believing that the automatic effect will be increased fitness amongst the family. Or would freely providing a Teletext and Prestel service for every home result in a more informed public? The point to be made is that neither educational progress nor curriculum improvement is a direct and inevitable consequence of technological advance.

A second issue is the order in which the introduction of the microcomputer in the classroom has occurred. Promoters of computer hardware, industry, and the Government through its subsidization scheme, may be portrayed as providing the initial definition of the value and use of a microcomputer in school. Such promoters may not be first concerned with the needs of teachers or the way in which the introduction of the microcomputer into classrooms can affect the curriculum process. A preferable approach may have been the prior consideration by practitioners of the improvements, enhancements and redirections needed in the curriculum that may possibly be engaged by recent technological advance. In view of the relatively large expenditure on subsidizing hardware a prior Commission of Inquiry or Consultative Committee Report might have set the horse before the cart.

As Weizenbaum has suggested (1), microcomputers have been so advanced in terms of hardware that they have solutions to which they are seeking problems. It may be that the introduction of the microcomputer into the education system is the best example of this contrapositioning. It is like a chemist delivering a range of medicines to doctors, who then have to decide what illnesses, if any, the medicines will suit. At classroom level the use to which the microcomputer is put is constrained by the imposition of specific hardware. The ends to which the hardware are engaged are defined by the means made available.

**Curriculum Models of Hardware Implementation**

When curriculum development occurs at a national level, three different ideologies may underpin the development. While these three ideologies are caricatures, it is noticable that the injection of microcomputers into schools is close to one of these, the 'Missionary' approach. The three approaches to curriculum development may be termed 'Missionary', 'Broker' and 'Executive'. One way of introducing computer hardware into the classroom may have been by a Broker approach. A Commission of Inquiry could have gathered together evidence from the widest variety of interested parties: teachers, parents, Inspectors, Advisors, Industry, Trade Unions and Professional Bodies to ascertain needs in terms of hardware and software. A Commission acting as a Broker would attempt to establish common ground between the various interest groups, reconciling, arbitrating and predicting. In terms of both hardware and software there appears to have been no such consultation.

An alternative method of introducing hardware and software into the classroom would have been via an 'Executive' approach. The rationale for this requires an historical perspective. Following the centralized curriculum developments in the 1960s and 1970s, much criticism was made of the centre-periphery model where development occurred at the centre and was disseminated outwards to the periphery (2). In particular, teachers adapted and changed the new curriculum materials to serve their own philosophy of practice. Such development may be perceived as a non-democratic control over curriculum content and culture. Central development may be regarded as a vehicle towards imposing on the majority the ideas of a minority. As alternative model therefore is for microcomputer hardware and software to be delivered in terms of the wants of practitioners. Recent movement towards school based or teacher based curriculum development urge change in the curriculum to occur at grass roots level. Expectation of a curriculum development capacity is invested in each individual school and each teacher. The role of central government is thereby relegated to an Executive one. Given the availability of money for hardware, schools under this model would define their needs, with central government responding in an Executive fashion.

A third method of introducing hardware and software into the classroom is by a 'Missionary' approach. The caricature of the Missionary approach is central government and its agencies believing that the introduction of the microcomputer into the classroom is a means of salvation for pupils, teachers and the curriculum. The evangelists of the computer revolution believe they have a special revelation of how to enrich the curriculum. The missionaries have a vision of teachers' needs which may be at variance with teachers' self expressed wants. A Missionary approach aims at converting as many as possible to the gospel of the microcomputer in the classroom.

Neither the Broker, the Executive or the Missionary approach is correct and the other two wrong. Each has in-built limitations. With a Broker approach, the introduction of computer hardware into classrooms may contain no unified and coherent philosophy. If the policies of consensus define the priorities, then what is acceptable to a majority may not constitute what is most valuable in terms of pupil growth and curriculum development. With the Executive approach, the limitation is that little progression in current practice may occur. To respond uncompromisingly to teacher wants may result in a stagnant and self-perpetuating curriculum, merely reproducing the customary and traditional. With the Missionary approach, there is the possibility of imposing grass skirts on naked, agnostic teachers. New clothes may be very attractive, they may be perceived as being able to transform personality and lifestyle, yet new clothes soon become worn, the novelty value soon wears off, and what is revealed at a later date is the imposition of counter-culture. Microcomputers

**111**

have been generously installed into classrooms and while not doubting the integrity and sincerity of the providers, sufficient and beneficial use on a scale large enough to justify the initial expense must be reviewed and evaluated.

## The Curriculum Implications of Program Production

Once the hardware is in school, how may the curriculum be affected? From hardware producers' advertisements and the proliferation of simple introductory books on writing programs, a teacher may well gain the impression that writing computer based learning (CBL) programs is as simple as writing a stencil or typing a letter. Yet the opposite is true in terms of software that truly creates curriculum development. Creating a program that can be rationally justified as creating re-direction and progression in the curriculum requires great labour and time. Neither of these commodities is available easily to the teacher. Gleason (3) has warned that development of good software requires careful specification of aims and objectives, analysis of the structure and sequence in a topic, drafts, trials, revisions and documentation. He points out that this is a very time-consuming and expensive process, well beyond the capability and resources of individuals and even small groups of teachers. It is therefore perhaps not surprising to find a flood of programs used in the classroom which are educationally poor. There is a strong argument for the idea of teacher produced material that is created and used "in-house". The translation of this idea into practice is disappointing when CBL is concerned. Simple rote exercises, tasks which would be better executed in a dynamic relationship with the teacher or in a small group situation, processes which lend themselves to the use of a variety of technologies, are all too quickly reduced to a computer program. There are maths programs which feed a repetative diet of basic number skills and foreign language programs which provide a tedious repetition of drill and practice in vocabulary and grammar. The quality of the diagnostic feedback and corrective information that a sensitive teacher can give far exceeds that of these programs.

Initially CBL programs may carry a mystique, an illusion of progression, a sense of being in the 21st century. To be a progressive teacher may mean being able to write, use or know about CBL programs. The microcomputer may be the teacher bandwagon of the 1980s. Once the mystique of the new technology is removed then many of the programs appear to be a step backwards in learning and teaching. For example, the way in which components of basic number processes are currently taught by CBL is more akin to the elementary school of the 19th century than the primary school of the 1980s.

Teachers and other authors of classroom software need to remove themselves from the novelty, mystique and illusion of skill given by CBL programs and evaluate their product rigorously in terms of its educational usefulness. Teachers who invest time and energy giving birth to a program may find it almost impossible to separate themselves from their product and test its real value in terms of the overall aim, content and process of the curriculum. Curriculum developments are normally evaluated before being introduced into the classroom. What appears to be lacking in the present production of CBL materials is precise, structured evaluation made widely available to inform users.

While the centre-periphery model of curriculum development is less fashionable at present, the CBL material that has been developed centrally appears outstanding in the company of that produced by individual teachers and software houses. Programs produced by the ITMA Project and the Computers in the Curriculum Project at Chelsea College may be examples of where curriculum enhancement has occurred. With both there is a recognizable educational philosophy underpinning production, there is considerable field testing before release and there is most importantly a prior concern to engage in curriculum development rather than mere program production.

### Curriculum Implications of CAI and CAL

The majority of maths, reading skills, modern language programs presently circulating follow a rote learning, drill and practice pattern which is exalted in computer jargon to the title of computer aided instruction (CAI). There are well rehearsed limitations of software which aim to instruct. These limitations may be listed as the underlying atomistic concept of knowledge, artificiality of reinforcement, loss of a dynamic interaction with the teacher, and the desirability of reducing all curriculum areas to a sequential structure.

Since instruction does not necessarily lead to learning, more enthusiasm may be generated by the practitioner for software which creates discovery learning, termed computer assisted learning (CAL). Simulating a dangerous chemistry experiment or a complex economic model of demand and supply has a great attraction, and doubtless can create an improved curriculum. The implicit danger is that laboratory experiments and field studies will all too quickly be translated into computer programs. It saves time, energy, organization and labour to run, for example, a conservation experiment on the computer. It may even make for easier classroom discipline. The danger is that pupils will be sold short on real practical involvement. There may be an over-reduction on field visits to test geographical or biological phenomena, or an over-reduction on experimentation with chemicals and living organisms in a laboratory. Is not first hand experience preferable to computer simulation? Computer simulation is a limited experience, limited by the medium of the message, limited to a minority of senses.

There is an additional issue which affects both CAI and CAL. The introduction and use of the microcomputer in the classroom may sometimes pevert the curriculum. The ease with which a floppy disk

**113**

can commence a lesson, the decrease in the amount of lesson preparation needed, the decrease in the need for exposition and marking may be seductive attributes of CBL. Thus, what is reducable to computer programs may be given more status. Areas of knowledge capable of computerization may be given a more central place in the curriculum. The production of educational software for the computer, posing as technological advance, may blurr the consideration of alternative forms of curriculum development.

## Implications for the Role of the Pupil

Any technology which creates individualized learning and makes the pupil more active is bound to be attractive. When the pupil appears to be in control of the speed and difficulty level of the program and when a one-to-one rather than thirty-to-one situation is possible, a child is likely to be more mentally active and learn more. This may be true. However, it also paradoxically appears to be the case that the child is made to be passive by CBL. The pupil is responding rather than initiating, reacting rather than inaugurating. The pupil becomes dependent on the program, being programmed by the microcomputer, rather than developing multi-experiential routes though a curriculum area. Is the outcome of this passivity that the pupil is less likely to develop confidence in personal knowledge, less likely to develop the ability to seek out knowledge from diverse sources? Is self-inquiry demoted as a skill, and responsivity and passivity promoted? If this is so, then passivity also has implications for the authority structure of the classroom. Technology which prescribes what is to be learnt, controls speed and difficulty level, judges the correctness of pupils' answers may contain a hidden curriculum. The pupil learns to accept authority and accepts an authoritative view of knowledge. The microcomputer appears to be legitimizing what is taught, what is correct and incorrect, with the consequential effect of pupils becoming passive recipients of authoritative knowledge. This may be very true of CAI and partially true of CAL. It is however, to the credit of LOGO that the reverse situation can exist, with children in control, programming the computer rather than being programmed by the computer, exploring their own ideas.

The role of the pupil is also affected by the type of communication that occurs with CBL programs. Software in classrooms mostly grossly truncates normal conversation. The computer can only operate on simple, predictable and recognizable responses by the pupil. An open conversation, a novel question, an unusual reply are not possible. It is therefore possible that the classroom microcomputer militates against natural language development.

It may be argued in response that the computer is not the only educational medium which creates passivity, an authoritative ideology and stultifies natural language development. Worksheets, workcards, chalk and talk, educational television all appear to do the same. The problem is that the microcomputer changes nothing. It does not create development and progress; rather it strengthens and reinforces existing approaches. Rather than inspiring teachers to re-examine their aims and goals in the curriculum, the microcomputer may act as a reactionary or confining influence on the curriculum.

## Implications for the Role of the Teacher

The carrot that is dangled before the teacher is the promise that the microcomputer will free the teacher for more time with individual pupils. This appears very desirable. However it reveals a deficiency. The teacher does not have enough time for individual contact. The microcomputer may provide a partial solution to this problem. But the real issue should be what cure is the more preferable: putting more machines into classrooms or more teachers? Assuming that teachers are more adaptable, versatile and flexible than the micro, the management problem may be best solved by increasing the supply of teachers in schools thereby reducing the pupil-teacher ratio. A teacher can be sensitive to pupils' ability, aptitude, attainment, attitude, sex, motivation and mood. The micro can barely take any of these into account. It is not only that the micro is a much inferior agent of learning compared with the teacher, but also its arrival in the classroom may hold back progress in obtaining an increased supply of teachers. Indeed it is possible that the introduction of microcomputers into schools lays a pathway for reduced manpower in the classroom.

The Industrial Revolution took away from many the unique and irreplaceable social life and vocational skills of the folk tradition. The Computer Revolution may detract from celebrating the unique and irreplaceable skills of the teacher. The Industrial Revolution led to a replacement of muscles by machinery. The Computer Revolution may lead to an attempted partial replacement of teachers' motivational and management skills by the microcomputer.

## Conclusion

Given the large expenditure on hardware and the investment of time and labour in software production, a comparable investment in evaluation seems warranted. As Wragg has observed "It is current policy to place a microcomputer in every school. Will anyone take the trouble to see whether in some small rural three-teacher primary school the teachers are favourably disposed to it, properly trained to exploit its potential, have enough software; will anyone enquire how it is actually used, or even whether the wretched machine is ever unwrapped?" (4).

In the 1970s the National Development Programme in Computer Assisted Learning was accompanied by the UNCAL evaluation (5) (6). A major evaluation thrust appears strikingly absent in the present UK programme. If an Executive stance had been taken in development, then a programme would find it imperative to evaluate teachers' reactions. If a Broker approach had been chosen then the various interest groups would all need to have been consulted. When a Missionary approach is adopted then the danger is that evaluation is relegated to a relatively inconsequential role. The vision of salvation is not to be clouded by the protestations of the unconverted. The underlying beliefs are not wrong and cannot be invalidated or changed. If the gospel message is unacceptable then the receivers need educating. To the Missionary, evaluation may be interesting, rarely informative, never directive. The evaluation may indicate the gap to be closed in in-service education. It will not indicate that the vision is wrong.

Few can doubt that the microcomputer is likely to change classroom practice or education in and out of school. In a time of rapid change there is the danger of being overtaken by the speed of that change, making evaluation an urgent priority. Evaluation best occurs in the midst of change rather than at the end of change.

The Missionary approach to recent microcomputer developments in education essentially involves a vision. The speed of development of the microcomputer has been dazzling. The surge in the production and distribution of CBL programs for the classroom can blind the gullible teacher. The result is an urgent need for supervision, for the critical eye of evaluation.

## REFERENCES

1.   Weizenbaum, J., Once more: the computer revolution. In Dertouzos, M.L. and Moses, J. (Eds.) *The Computer Age: A Twenty Year View.* MIT Press, Cambridge, Massachusetts (1979).

2.   MacDonald, B. & Walker, R., *Changing the Curriculum,* Open Books, London (1976).

3.   Gleason, G.T., Microcomputers in Education: The State of the Art, *Educational Technology, 21,* 7 (1981).

4.   Wragg, T., From research into action. *British Educational Research Journal, 8,* 3 (1982).

5.   Kemmis, S., How do Students Learn? CARE Occasional Publication No. 5, UEA, Norwich (1978).

6.   MacDonald, B. et al, The Programme at Two. CARE, UEA, Norwich (1975).

# COMPUTERS AND THE TEACHING OF WRITING: PROSE AND POETRY

Stephen Marcus

## The Composing Process

The act of writing can serve two purposes. First, it can serve to *record* what one knows. In this regard, it is most familiar in the schools as a means for documenting pupils' acquisition of knowledge in the form of essay tests, end of term examinations, etc. A very different conception of writing, however, is that it is a means for *discovering* what it is one may come to understand. In this sense, writing is a learning tool, and it can be used as a formative instrument in any discipline to help learn better what the specific curriculum mandates.

Whether in the service of recording or discovery, the composing process can be usefully divided into three stages: pre-writing (P), writing (W), and re-writing (R). Pre-writing includes thinking about the topic, making notes, false starts, early drafts, talking ideas over with others and using idea-generating strategies (e.g., freewriting, clustering, brain-storming). The *writing* stage consists of putting down the "final" version of the piece. Re-writing includes re-working the piece after some perspective has been attained. It also includes editing and proofreading. It has been noted that professional writers probably spend 85% of their time pre-writing, 1% writing and 14% re-writing (1). Many "writer's blocks" disappear when people stop trying to edit a passage they haven't even pre-written yet.

The P-W-R process is, of course, not simply a sequence of these stages. It is a recursive process. The writer is involved in different stages depending on which portion of the total piece he/she is working on. A concluding paragraph may have been completely finished before the introductory paragraph has been pre-written.

Computers not only can reduce the overall amount of time spent on a writing task but can alter the quantity and quality of time spent during any given stage.

## Invisible Writing with Computers

Many teachers have long advocated the practice of "freewriting" as a technique for developing fluency and as an appropriate tool in the prewriting stage of the composing process. The emphasis in freewriting is on the flow of thought rather than on immediate attention to the details of grammar, spelling, punctuation, etc. Recent experiments we have been conducting suggest that word processors can provide a special environment for freewriting (2). Simply by adjusting the brightness of their monitors, pupils may eliminate immediate visual feedback yet still be recording their ideas. The text may eventually be examined by brightening the screen display, and as usual, it is available for editing, saving, and later printing. Pupils commonly reported that when they wrote under ordinary circumstances, they usually allowed their minds to wander; rarely did they keep their attention focused undeviatingly on a single train of thought for more than one or two sentences. In addition, pupils noted that their usual pattern in composing was to interrupt the flow of thought frequently to edit and amend the language, syntax, and mechanics of their developing text. Invisible writing experiments suggested to them that their usual pauses obstructed their fluency and, more importantly, diluted their concentration. Under the conditions of the experiment, they could neither edit nor rewrite, nor allow their attention to stray from the line of thought they were developing.

Invisible writing with computers discouraged the kind of "local editing" which is particularly common with word processors and which is counterproductive at certain stages of the composing process. It encouraged a quality of attention to the topic at hand which is sometimes lacking in normal free-writing activities. Not everyone, of course, found it a congenial procedure, even after practice. Still, for many pupils invisible writing helped them see how premature editing interfered with their writing, and it brought into sharp relief their own personal tendencies and compulsions in this regard. In the words of one pupils, "invisible writing helped me understand that writing really begins with prewriting."

**The Moving Cursor Having Writ ...**

... can erase or copy all of it. The cursor, that blinking pulse of the machine, can do much more, of course, depending on the particular system being used. A significant event in our computer literacy workshops for English and language arts teachers is the participants' first experience with their power over the cursor. Their ability to "physically" move through words without altering them is often the teachers' first experience with the fluidity of videotext (the term is discussed at more length below). It is a significant experience, as is invisible writing, for developing an awareness of the actual relationships between what they see on the screen and what they will eventually get. It helps them acquire the perspective which allows a writer, or teacher of writing, to fully exploit the medium.

One of the earliest to adapt the technology to writing instruction was James Joyce, then at the University of California, Berkeley (3). At that time Joyce's pupils were using a wordprocessing system which automatically filled out the lines when the text was printed. Lines displayed on the screen could be of any length; when a printed copy was produced, the space on each line was automatically filled with text and justified. Joyce recommended that pupils enter their text a phrase to a line. Aside from making later editing easier, this method allowed pupils more easily to notice whether their phrases tended in general to be too long or short, helped the writers focus on intact semantic units, and encouraged syntactic maturity in conjunction with sentence-combining activities. Joyce also suggested that in some cases of writer's block, the simple act of scrolling text up the screen "....literally got things moving again. This has worked successfully when all that was being formatted was the title, name of the author, and the author's address."

Seeing words dance around the screen - with procedures and special function keys like search-and-replace, move text, delete, retype - generates quite a different sense for many pupils of the "risk" in committing themselves to writing. They no longer feel their words to be "carved in stone" (often the stone of writer's block). Instead, their words now have the quality of light. Children can see their sentences slide back and forth, ripple down the screen, disappear, reappear, be highlighted, etc. For example, one of the practice files we have developed is based on a "first line/last line" idea. When pupils load the SCREEN SCENES file into their word processor, they see two apparently unrelated sentences, for example:

> He checked his schedule to see what he planned to ruin today. They left him wondering whether the door would close in time.

The directions are to move the cursor between the sentences and to type in a story which connects them. As they do, they see the second (i.e., final) sentence creep to the right, snaking down the screen as they continue typing. If they can develop a coherent sequence of events before the concluding sentence "disappears" off the bottom of the screen, all the better. It's not a necessary objective, but it proves to be an interesting and challenging one. Exercises like this provide opportunities for practicing cursor control, coherence, unity, etc. They also immerse the pupil in the medium's more subtle message: their words are not fixed and rigid. Expression has shape and movement - literally and figuratively.

### Making the Implicit Explicit

While activities like freewriting attempt to turn the inner voice *off* in the service of fluency, some researchers are attempting to turn it *up* in order to study and perhaps train it. This is the composing-out-loud technique used for example by Janet Emig (4). There are intriguing relationships between the transcripts of such sessions and the records generated by computer-assisted prewriting tutorials. Such tutorials include Schwartz's SEEN program for exploring topics

**119**

in literature; Burns' three heuristic programs based on Aristotle's *Topoi*, and Wresch's Essay Writer, which helps pupils develop the substance of different kinds of essays but does the formatting and paragraph construction by itself **(5).** Additionally, Rubin and colleagues have developed computer-assisted activities to help children write stories, while our own work has included courseware for helping pupils (age 11 years and up) study and write poetry **(6).**

While the composing-out-loud research has attempted to elicit the writer's own inner dialogue, computer-assisted tutorials such as the ones cited above - although not necessarily designed with this in mind - may be looked upon as attempts to create a sort of ideal inner dialogue (or the kind of productive office hour that teachers dream about). The hope is occasionally expressed that pupils will eventually internalize the procedures and not merely rely on the machines for guidance. In these tutorials, the computer (not a word processor in the usual sense of the phrase) provides the effective problem-solving strategies and positive feedback which are so noticeably absent in so many of the research transcripts, which are instead filled with "irrelevant" or counter-productive inner dialogue and self-generated negative feedback. By virtue of using such computer-assisted tutorials, pupils are provided with an immediate transcript, a kind of composing-out-loud protocol to serve as record and resource for future drafts.

Along with procedures for peer-editing, we have been experimenting with computer-assinged collegial prewriting, again utilizing the special attributes of the medium. In this case, we have tried combining a modified version of invisible writing with the "writing consultant" approach implicit in the tutorials discussed above. Our word processing systems run on microcomputers which have video monitors connected by a wire to the actual keyboard/computer. We simply have students sitting next to each other exchange monitors, so that for example Student A's monitor (still connected to Student A's computer) rests atop Student B's computer. Student B's monitor rests on Student A's computer. The monitors are angled slightly to discourage peeking. As Student A begins prewriting on a topic, the text appears in front of Student B. If Student A loses the train of thought, he or she types "???" whereupon Student B types a response such as "You were talking about...." If Student A runs out of ideas, he or she types "XXX." Student B may then suggest a new line of thought or an additional perspective on A's current thought. Student A may use the suggestion or not, as appropriate. When the students print their respective files, Student A has the text, and Student B has the record of assistance. The two files together constitute a record of collaboration for further study and discussion and for use in Student A's next draft.

This kind of activity utilizes the advantages of freewriting and invisible writing, adding to them the benefits of training students to be careful readers, paraphrasers, and writing consultants. Students are writing for an audience which actually responds to the meaning of their text - something which the tutorials do not do. While this application of invisible writing is in certain ways not nearly as productive as the tutorials, the procedure does have benefits not available with such programs, not the least of which is that it helps maintain in a very real way the social dimension of the composing process and the sense of audience. It also provides a temporary antidote to the isolation some people feel when working with computers.

## Pruning the Trees, Shaping the Forest

There exist several quite powerful revision and editing programs which will read a pupil's paper and provide information on sentence type, paragraph structure, wordiness and use of cliches, readability, use of passive voice and nominalization, sentence-length variability, etc. Teachers overburdened with 500-word themes to grade may react with some ambivalence to the knowledge that a computer can process a paper in less time than it takes to read this sentence. IBM's Epistle, Westinghouse's Writing Aids System and Bell Laboratories' Writer's Workbench are examples of programs designed to improve writing by examining text, providing feedback on surface structure, and suggesting improvements.

Text analysis programs such as the ones mentioned above are machine-specific, and only a few are available for microcomputers. In addition, while some are very fast, others are quite slow (by computing standards). Still, the speed with which a word processor can accomplish even a global search-and-replace (SAR) instills a significant number of people with a new sense of power over their writing, a particularly important sense of power when it comes to editing and revising their text.

One of our demonstration/practice files, SHERLOCK, consists of a passage from a Sherlock Holmes story in which certain vowels have been replaced by symbols (there is an additional substitution to make things interesting). This results in a rather long series of lines which seem at first glance to be total nonsense as they scroll up the screen. For example:

7nxgl!nc7ngx?v$rxmyxn?t$sx?fxth$S$v-
(and so on for some 70 lines)

The task is to decode the file by practicing global SAR procedures, i.e., having the computer search for every occurance of a given symbol and replace it with the indicated vowel. Since this activity often occurs in workshop settings with no written instructions for instituting an SAR, the participants are led through one or two substitutions to teach them the key-press procedures. When asked to count the number of seconds required for the first substitution to actually take place, there is predictable amazement when they see it completed before anyone reaches "One." It has happened before they have quite understood that it *could* have happened.

**121**

A more "practical" revision example is to have the workshop participants load the THREE TO ONE file which consists of a narrative passage written in third person singular. The task is to transform it to first person singular using only four SAR procedures. Although this activity, along with ones like SHERLOCK, are designed to demonstrate and practice specific key-press sequences and editing functions, their major initial effect is to immerse the novice in an environment in which the computer does tricks with words. They serve to illustrate Arthur C. Clarke's adage that "any sufficiently advanced technology is indistinguishable from magic." It is the attraction to this "magic show" which Gould has suggested keeps writers experienced with word processors fiddling with their text (7). Others have noted that local editing of words and sentences can interfere with ongoing composing. Perhaps this focus inhibits the broader perspective needed for reconceptualizing larger units or for altering stylistic features. It is this broader perspective that is provided by the text analysis programs mentioned earlier, which although sometimes relatively limited in scope, are constantly being made more sophisticated and accessible. Even without access to one of these analysis programs, it is still possible to provide this larger perspective, for example with SAR procedures similar to those described above. In one case, a teacher working with twelve year old pupils had been using a word processor with them for months but had not thought to have them work with SAR. A brief experience with SHERLOCK and THREE TO ONE was all she needed to begin her own creative applications, for example, in having pupils' poems about plant life cycles become transformed into poems about their own.

## Computers and Poetry

The linking of computers, poets, and poetry occurs in at least five regards: 1) poetry written with the aid of word processors, 2) poetry written on the subject of computers, 3) poetry redefined in terms of the computer-aided procedures used to produce it, 4) computer-generated poetry, and 5) poetry written with interactive software which guides the form and content of the poem. In an effort to explore the last-named approach, I have been developing a language arts activity called Compupoem, an activity which gives pupils an opportunity to use a computer while they study and write poetry.

Compupoem prompts the user for different parts of speech and formats the words in a haiku-like poetic structure. The writer may then select from fourteen different kinds of advice on such things as choosing adverbs, prepositional phrases, nouns, etc., and on zen and the art of computer use. Pupils may also see their poems instantly re-written in different formats in order to examine the relationship between form and impact. Compupoem is quite different from programs which generate random sequences of poetic phrases. Instead, it elicits the pupil's knowledge and imagination in a more active involvement in the writing.

The process is also different in important ways from "fill in the blanks" activities like Mad-Libs; in which the user's words are inserted into a pre-determined template. Compupoem requires that the child supply both the parts and the overall conception of the whole. In addition, while most word games and drill-and-practice activities are won by the user's coming up with the correct answers, Compupoem tries to encourage the attitude that "winning" results from producing interesting answers.

Compupoem has been used with school children and with out-of-school adults from a variety of backgrounds (including professional poets). The authors of the poems below range from high school pupils to unversity professors.

### Cathi's Poem

The sonata for eyes
    magenta, secretive
        side-stepped through their dreams
           stealthily, with sorrow.

### Paul's Poem

The riveter
Brawny, sweatcaked at Miller Time
Carefully slouches
Bethlehembound

### Sheridan's Poem

The words
    masterful, serving
for inspiration
    gently, insistently
solace.

### Diane's Poem

Love
    tender, life-giving
hidden from sight
    patiently, forever
waiting.

### Marla's Poem

The tree house
    full of childhood memories
suspended on the lonely oak tree
    softly, in a whisper
swaying.

### Compupoem and the Writing Process

In certain respects, Compupoem did not do anything that any classroom teacher could not have done: it simply gave directions and advice. In other respects, however, its computer-assisted dimensions provided unique occasions for exploring each stage of the composing process.

To begin with, the prompts which the instructions provided (a sequence of requests for certain parts of speech) constituted a heuristic device for generating both the subject of the poem and its substance. The procedure encouraged fairly rapid and copious prewriting of poems - and while quantity did not always engender quality, the ease with which "first drafts" could be produced proved to be a significant factor for those for whom writing did not come easily and especially for those who had little idea of how to begin writing a poem.

While the prompts, appearing as they did in a somewhat alien context (i.e., on a computer screen), aided in pre-writing, the actual "writing" of the poem was accomplished in an instant. The pupils saw a list of ideas suddenly transformed into a poetic whole. Whether or not it was a satisfying or "correct" version of a pupil's overall idea and intent, this first draft provided more refined raw material than did the list of ideas or qualities which the prompts elicited.

Before the children were presented with the Advice Option menu, they were encouraged to write their poems on paper before proceeding. Not having the computer simply store the first version derived from a concerted attempt to have the children "re-own" their words and poems, to take back responsibility for shaping the poems by revising in the course of recording. In this regard, it was interesting to note the responses of pupils to the following evaluation question:

> Who wrote your poem? (circle your choice)
> (you) 1    2    3    4    5    (the computer)

Children tended to circle higher numbers for early poems and lower numbers for later ones. The degree to which they felt that both the form and the content of their poems were suggestive indicators of the nature of the composing process.

While there did exist an Advice Option which would re-write the poem in different ways, it was thought important to retain and encourage the pupils' involvement in immediate decisions about revising the poem. They soon learned that one of the "rules of the game" was that if they did not value their work enough to write it down, it would disappear. They would lose the chance to reconsider their words. It thus provided a new kind of object-lesson in valuing themselves.

It might be interesting to provide here an example of a poem which emerged from a pre-written draft.

### Harold's Poem

> The reptilian brain
>     sweet, juicy
> in the nick of time's swamp
> gracelessly
> beckons.

Here is the poem written after the one above. While it is obviously not just an expanded version of the first, it was clearly engendered by the earlier pre-writing. Also, the writer obviously did not limit himself to "filling in the prompts."

### Harold's Apple in Eden

Sleek sensual in its robust, organized plastic,
inviting to the finger
    (and hence the nerves of the arm, the brain,
    the great outdoors),
etched in religious hues and mystical language
    (data, terminal, yes, no)
the future reptile slinks happily
through our lives.

### Zen and the Art of Compupoem

In the course of developing Compupoem, we have encountered a few people whose reactions suggested that we should include some elements which addressed the issues of computer anxiety, the nature of poetry, and the definition of a poet. Adapting some familiar advice, we included the following Advice Option under the title, "Zen". Upon selecting that option, the pupils would see this videotext:

This may or may not apply to you...but RELAX!!!

Some people struggle with this game (i.e., the computer).
They compete with it or feel themselves terribly constrained by its rules or by their own sense of what "poetry" is.

Take a tipe from some ancient Zen wisdom:

In the beginning, the computer is the master.
Then, the person is master of the computer.
In the end, neither needs to be master.

If that doesn't inspire you, nothing will.

Time to get back to work...

Want to write another poem?

Some children have had fascinating and fruitful objections to Compupoem. The writing it produced, according to one pupil, could not be a poem because the machine did the writing, with the pupil merely producing "words in answer to the computer's questions." Such objections provided wonderful opportunities for raising such

**125**

questions as "What is a poem? What is a poet? Having used Compupoem, are you now a poet (not necessarily a good poet, but a poet)? How do you know? What does a set of words need, how does it need to have been produced, in order for it to be considered poetry?" These questions are part of the stock-in-trade of any English teacher. They were given new power in the context of pupils' personal involvement in creating "poems" which were challenged as such by their peers. Class evaluations of such discussions suggest that they were valuable in generating new and broader insights into the creative process.

Another interesting aspect of children's approach to Compupoem relates to their differing cognitive styles. Some children built up their poems part by part (literally, part of speech) using inductive, detail-oriented strategies. In the words of one pupil, she was "...amazed at how the words that seemed so separate fit together so well". Other pupils began with an overall, intuitive, visual sense of the whole of their conception and then filled in the missing parts (of speech): "I tried to visualize what the eventual outcome of the poem would be and to think of words or phrases that would make the poem more interesting" or "When I chose my words... the thought was not particularly well-developed. It was part of an image in my mind".

As children grew accustomed to the technology, they more often than not let their own styles determine their approach. They were also more able to freely revise the form and content when they recorded their work. Pupils have reported that Compupoem elicited concerns for planning ahead, unity and coherence. Many enjoyed being "quizzed" on parts of speech in a non-judgmental, puzzle-like setting. And there was, of course, that unique quality of a computer that seemed to capture the attention of non-writers and transform them into writers.

### Reading, Writing, and Videotext: Some Concluding Remarks

A good deal of what has been considered here revolves around what pupils see (or do not see) on their screens. There are indications that print which appears on television screens is neither print, per se, nor television. Rather, it is print-on-television: a new medium with its own characteristic messages. In a study of children and electronic text - what is being called here "videotext" - Paisley and Chen suggest that while television "undermined the functional basis of literacy... the technologies (of electronic text systems) depend *more* on literacy than even print media. At the same time, it is possible that intrinsically motivating aspects of electronic text use may cause children to read more, and at an earlier age" **(8)**.

It may perhaps be true that word processors designed especially for pupils owe their success in part to the fact that they are easy for *teachers* to learn (it is of note that eleven and twelve year olds can quite easily master a relatively complex system like 'Apple Writer'). Nevertheless, it is the chance to play with the technology which may prove to be of primary importance in pupils' willingness to develop computer-assisted writing skills. This intrinsically motivating aspect of computers in general, and of videotext specifically, deserves special attention and study. Seminal work on what makes computer games fun has been done by Malone **(9)**. His discussions of challenge, fantasy, and curiosity in connection with computer games can enrich and inform any development of computer-assisted writing instruction, from arcade-style word games and skill-building activities to more sedate and cerbral exercises like the SCREEN SCENES assignment described previously.

Videotext generates interesting questions about reading from and writing for television screens. Several researchers are examining how instructional text should appear on the screen (a screenful at a time, in semantic units, in units changing from a word to a phrase depending on the person's reading level?). And who should control the speed at which the words appear? The reader? The teacher? The computer, based on the reader's response time? If parts of speech can be colour-coded, as they already can be to a certain extent, will it help some pupils if we "paint" a passage from Hemingway and compare it to the mosaic produced by a passage from Faulkner? This gives new meaning to the words "language arts," and it might be a boon to the more visually oriented children in their attempts to discern an author's style. Will it help to paint successive drafts of some pupils' essays, so they can see in a new way how their writing may be changing?

As more people's jobs involve writing "readable TV" - computer-assisted instruction, electronic mail, teletext and viewdata systems, captioned TV - what will the effects be on reading and writing behaviour? Harold Innis noted in *The Bias of Communication* that "the use of a new medium of communication over a long period will to some extent determine the character of knowledge to be communicated". Individuals who already are practiced in creating videotext are finding that writing for television screens alters their sense of the structure of knowledge and of the language conventions used to express it. They experience demands for a degree of visual and design awareness which they did not initially possess. Spelling, punctuation, and paragraph structure are altered to conform to the limitations (or perhaps strengths) of the medium **(10)**.

All this may seem far afield from the initial considerations of how computers can be used in writing classes. Such considerations are grounded, however, in the almost galvanic "jump for joy", the actual physical response evidenced by many people when they first see their words dancing on the screen, not carved in stone, but electric and fluid. Neil Postman, discussing information environments in *Teaching as a Conserving Activity*, notes that there are important consequences to changing the form of information, its quantity, or speed, or direction. Teachers and pupils involved in computer-assisted writing instruction are helping shape a new environment even as they are being shaped by it.

# REFERENCES

1. Murray, D.M., Teaching Writing as a Process, Not Product, *The Leaflet*, New England Assoc. of Teachers of English (November, 1972).

2. Marcus, S. and Blau, S., Invisible Writing With Computers, *Educational Technology* (in press).

3. Joyce, J., UNIX Aids for English Composition Courses, Paper presented at the Western Educational Computing Conference, San Francisco (1981).

4. Emig, J., The Composing Process of Twelfth Graders, National Council of Teachers of English, Urbana, Illinois (1971).

5. Schwartz, H., A Computer Program for Intervention and Audience Feedback, Paper presented at the Conference on College Composition and Communication, San Francisco (1982).

   Burns, H., Stimulating Intervention in English Composition Through Computer-Assisted Instruction, *Educational Technology, 20* (1980).

   Wresch, W., Computers in English Class: Finally Beyond Grammar and Spelling Drills, *College English, 44*, 5(1982).

6. Rubin, A., Making Stories, Making Sense, *Language Arts* (1980).

   Marcus, S., The Muse and the Machine: A Computers and Poetry Project, *Classroom Computer News* (November/December, 1982).

7. Gould, J., Composing Letters with Computer Based Text Editors, *Human Factors, 23*, 5(1981).

8. Paisley, W., and Chen, M., Children and Electronic Text: Challenges and Opportunities, in New Literacy, NIE Studies, Institute for Communication Research (April 1982).

9. Malone, T.W., Toward a Theory of Intrinsically Motivating Instruction, *Cognitive Science, 4* (1981).

10. see for example, Winsburg, R., *The Electronic Bookstall*, International Institute of Communications, London (1979).

# MICROCOMPUTERS AND THE ENGLISH TEACHER

Daniel Chandler

## Computer Literacy

Few English teachers would dispute the need for children to learn about computers, but most would deny that it is any concern of theirs. There is a real danger, therefore, that where opportunities do exist in schools for children to learn about computers no attention will be paid to developing an awareness of the computer as an emerging mass medium, requiring skills which are in some ways extensions to the traditional literacy skills with which English teachers have been concerned - reading, writing and fact-finding.

Screen-reading, keyboard and retrieval skills are not the same as reading, writing and fact-finding with other media (I). And yet so far "computer literacy" courses in schools have tended, ironically, to concentrate on the technology rather than on the medium. Children may quickly become fluent in using a keyboard and reacting to prompts from a screen with daunting speed without any help from adults, but to assume that they are "aware" of the medium and have acquired, for instance, efficient reading and information retrieval skills through use alone would leave them at a considerable disadvantage.

Computers are far more part of the everyday lives of children (and adults) than their present distribution in schools might suggest, and however well-designed educational programs may be, children need to be able to cope with reading many kinds of screen displays for a variety of purposes. It may not take us long to familiarise ourselves with new reading conventions (if we have the opportunity) but English teachers really ought to be involved in helping to develop efficient reading strategies using a medium which is rapidly becoming a more routine resource for up-to-date information than print.

Critical as it is, this is only one of the reasons why I feel English teachers should be playing a more active part in educational computing. A small but increasing number are just beginning to discover some of the possibilities of the microcomputer as a flexible new classroom resource. The most useful applications in English might be classified under four headings describing the role of the computer:

- A Writer's Workshop
- A Research Machine
- A Reading Glass
- A Framework for Talk

**Writer's Workshop**

I remember distinctly the first time I read a particular passage in Seymour Papert's revolutionary book MINDSTORMS which struck a chord in me as an English teacher. He was making a case for the use of the computer as a writing instrument, and one sentence reflected a major concern of my own. "For most children", he wrote, "rewriting a text is so laborious that the first draft is the final copy, and the skill of reading with a critical eye is never acquired" (2). Regarding the computer as an editing machine, I suddenly realised that English teachers could hardly have hoped for a better ally in helping young writers. Few children enjoy the process of drafting with pen and paper, but I have yet to find a child who does not take a delight in doing so with a word-processor.

The general advantages of the computer as a writing instrument are already well-documented, but it may be useful here to refer to widespread findings about the particular usefulness of word-processors for children. Perhaps the most important is that young writers are less inhibited by the thought of making mistakes: they no longer need to be confronted by their own insistent reminders of a stream of false starts. Speeding up this crucial stage of what has been described as "pre-writing" is a great encouragement to reluctant writers. Secondly, because of the professional quality of the presentation, they are able to take a far greater pride in their writing. They also tend to be much more keen to experiment and revise their writing if they do not have to face (or decide against) rewriting entire pages in order to make improvements to their texts. It is as easy to reorganise large sections of text as to correct a single spelling. It is hardly surprising, therefore, that children have been found to produce more extended texts using computers. Finally, contrary to popular expectations, writing with computers in schools is a very social activity: without the barrier of handwriting, children are far more keen to write with, and share their writing with, other children.

Those English teachers who have had the good fortune to be amongst the privileged few who have so far been able to experiment with word-processors need little convincing as to their usefulness for their purposes. Whilst it is true that at the time of writing microcomputers are still too scarce in schools for all children to use them with sufficient regularity to make any dramatic impact on their writing, to ignore their increasing availability in schools on a scale already far exceeding that of typewriters would be short-sighted indeed. I would hazard a guess that within only a few years most English departments will be involved in the routine use of word-processing packages.

My choice of the term "Writer's Workshop" was, however, intended to include not only word-processing, but also other "writer's aids". Few programs which fall into this category are as yet easily available in schools, but several major programs in this area will be released fairly soon. It may be helpful to have some idea of what kind of software can be expected.

George Keith at the North Cheshire Language Centre is at present developing a program which I shall refer to as WORDHOARD (it lacks an official name at present) (3). Designed for the Middle School age-range, it springs from a desire to help children to develop their vocabulary not by learning decontextualised lists of words but by consciously searching for words for specific purposes. More experienced writers may find aids such as Roget's Thesaurus helpful for such purposes, but for children the material and the arrangement is far too remote from their experience. The program is not to be simply a computer-based wordbank of synonyms, but also a guide in the search for alternative words. Initially the wordbank would be empty. The program provides guidance in how to search for alternative words and the child then feeds in her discoveries, and those she considers related to it in the wordbank. The computer stores this growing hoard for continual reuse and extension, providing not only a valuable tool for a group of young writers, but a unique map of a voyage of linguistic discovery which is of considerable use to the teacher too. At a later stage in the development of the program George Keith hopes to be able to build into the program a capability to manipulate the data so gathered in order to draw from it guidelines to a variety of activities built around the classification and creative use of words. Mike Sharples of the University of Edinburgh has been developing software which allows us to regard the computer as "a construction kit for language" which can offer children an opportunity to engage in linguistic research (4). WALTER (Word ALTERer) allows the user to experiment with grammatical transformations of text. She can type in a story, for instance, and then see the effect of transformations such as deleting every occurrence of particular parts of speech, changing a sentence into the passive voice, and, perhaps most powerfully, combining short sentences using relative clauses.

An example of how this powerful combining feature works is as follows. The initial text might be this:

"Once there was a pretty princess. The princess lived in a big castle in a forest. The forest was dark. She was very lonely because she has no friends to play with."

Typing the command **RELATIVE** would change the text to this:

"Once there was a pretty princess who lived in a big castle in a dark forest. She was very lonely because she had no friends to play with." This facility alone would of course be a very powerful tool indeed for a child who, like so many, experiences considerable difficulty in progressing from disjointed sentences to a more fluid style. But at a more advanced level the program will allow users to experiment with their own models of language by creating new commands, having devised the rules on which they are to be based.

Such programs, when they become available for schools in the near future, will allow us, in the words of Anthony Adams (until recently chair of the National Association for the Teaching of English) "to change dramatically the things which we as English teachers are concerned with" (5).

**Research Machine**

I have referred already to the importance of developing appropriate skills for computer-based information retrieval as an essential part of "computer literacy". Simply as a resource, as with the word-processor, computerized information systems should be of interest to English teachers.

There are already several information-handling programs available for microcomputers in schools, the best-known being AUCBE's QUERY (and ILEA's related program, LEEP). But the use of such software in schools has already received considerable attention in print, and I would like to introduce the topic to English teachers from a slightly different angle.

TREE OF KNOWLEDGE is a program which has recently been released by Acornsoft for the BBC Microcomputer (a similar program called SEEK, developed by Jon Coupland and the ITMA collaboration, will soon be available for a variety of machines). It was designed as a simple but flexible introduction to information handling on microcomputers, but with a focus on developing classification trees in science subjects. Despite this intention, it has considerable potential in the language arts.

Essentially, it allows the user either to create or to search through a tree of questions. These questions can either be used as a method of classification, as in developing a key to wild flowers, or as the basis for a guessing game. The game option derives from the famous computer game called ANIMAL, in which a human player plays Twenty Questions with the computer trying to guess which animal she is thinking of. As many readers will know, if the computer fails to "guess" correctly the user "teaches" it both the name of the creature and a yes/no question in order to help it guess successfully in future - a very motivating activity in itself.

As a small-group activity this has been found to have great value for language development - users are forced to ask more and more subtle questions which make increasingly nice distinctions. And in the process they soon need to resort to dragging relevant information from all available sources. In the case of printed texts this leads to both extensive and intensive reading, when such raw information must be shaped into usable yes/no questions. This, it seems to me, involves true "comprehension" and is infinitely more useful than exercises in reading recall.

TREE OF KNOWLEDGE and SEEK allow this game to be played with any subject-matter, but the computer begins by knowing nothing at all, so some sort of tree must be built up before a game can be played. In addition, you are allowed to see on the screen or to print on paper the tree itself - with its branches, questions and objects, allowing users, for instance, to explore the *"language in use"* theme of the way in which language can classify information into trees.

As with most cases for the use of computers in education, I feel, the argument is not that the same content could not be appraoched in a similar way *without* a microcomputer, but that the management issues for the teacher so often loom too large to make the activity as rich and worthwhile. In fact, all too often these difficulties mean that no such activity is undertaken at all.

## Reading Glass

I have chosen the metaphor of a "reading glass" to cover software which allows us to use the computer to help us to focus on texts. CLUES was developed by the ITMA Collaboration in Plymouth. It enables users (usually intitially the teacher) to enter texts into the computer, and then to display them on the screen in a variety of altered ways. One such way is, of course, the classic Cloze procedure, with the deletion of say, every tenth word. But there are many computerised versions of Cloze procedure, and most of them are typical of the robotic programs which put so many English teachers off the idea of using computers at all. Such versions of Cloze can destroy the whole point of the activity by marking as "correct" or "incorrect" the suggestions which users offer.

CLUES simply displays a text, with the chosen modifications, such as deletions, so it's a very flexible learning aid rather than a device for monitoring a mechanical exercise. It's entirely up to the user to decide how to use it, although one must admit that some teachers prefer to use programs which are less demanding of them and more self-contained.

CLUES is suitable for more than just Cloze. It can cope with a variety of techniques for masking or highlighting text: individual letters within words may be scrambled, for instance. Words within sentences - and paragraphs or verses - can also be jumbled. Such facilities can be used to help to develop sequencing skills. Phrases can be highlighted in different colours - which may sound trivial but which is a fascinating and easy technique for tracing themes in a poem (ITMA reported considerable success with using this feature to trace - in blue and red - two contrasting messages in a political

**133**

speech). In short, CLUES can offer ways of helping users to *focus* on texts.

DEVELOPING TRAY is a program which is being developed by Bob Moy at Chelsea College. It looks at first like a rather drastic Cloze exercise. Short texts are presented with only the punctuation visible, and students are asked if they can "bring up" the message in the "developing tray" by predicting individual letters, words and phrases. The activity can be played as a game with small groups of pupils since it uses a points system which has been found to be very popular. Asking for letters, words and phrases to be shown costs the player points, but successful prediction gains them. The scoring system is weighted in favour of predicting larger units than single letters, so there is an incentive to think about the cohesion of the passage as a whole rather than simply showing off any ability one might already have to recognise familiar letter patterns.

This is in my opinion an excellent variation on Cloze procedure, and as a program has the unusual but useful feature of a "scratchpad" which is used by the pupils during the course of a game to record their evolving speculations about the subject and meaning of the passage (usually a poem), once again reinforcing the real value of such an activity as a way of focussing attention on themes as well as structures in texts. Its greatest strength, it seems to me, is that such a program does not merely make an existing approach to literature more effective, but that it makes possible a new learning strategy. Texts which might previously have been thought "too difficult" for a particular age-group can with this game be tackled without any teacher direction at all. A printout of the group's developing ideas at the end of a session could be a very valuable piece of literary criticism which a group might have been quite unable or at least unwilling to attempt in any other way.

**Framework for Talk**

Those who are unfamiliar with the effect of computers in the classroom may think it perverse to suggest that the use of the computer can promote constructive discussion rather than inhibit it. Many English teachers who are new to the technology have nightmare visions of silent rows of children in cubicles staring mindlessly and hollow-eyed at so-called "educational games " with names such as SPELL-INVADERS or CAPS-MAN. But all the research studies undertaken so far show that this is far from being the case. In practice the use of the micro as a learning resource has been found to lead to an increase in useful talk and collaborative activities, even in classes where such activities were already encouraged (6).

Computer-managed simulations in particular can both create opportunities for and add purpose to informal group discussion. They can make possible a genuine discussion of possibilities which might normally result in posturing rather than real thinking, in cliches rather than exploratory talk. I have been impressed by examples I have seen where the assistance which the computer can offer in structuring such activities has provided a chance for teachers to use simulation when they might otherwise have lacked the confidence to do so. For once the teacher is able to be a friendly, observant participant in a learning situation where there are no right answers, only possibilities to be explored. One of the concerns of English teachers is to encourage informal group discussion so that pupils may explore ideas and ways of expressing them; one of their problems is the setting up of situations where such talk can happen without their own involvement. With the use of computer-managed simulations, not only is the teacher freed of the direct management of the group, but *pupils may be freed from the teacher* so that such talk can occur.

There are a number of simulation programs in the field of the Humanities which are of use to the English teacher in this sense, but I would like to focus on a rather different kind of simulation software.

As I have argued elsewhere, (7) many of the currently available ADVENTURE programs which are intended for single-player home entertainment have considerable potential as a focus for language activities with mixed-ability English groups. Many readers will know the genre, but briefly players find themselves in locations which are described in words on the screen, and their goal is to explore the landscape and solve whatever problems they discover by typing in commands to the computer such as "GO INTO THE ROOM" or "OPEN THE BOX".

Used with a group, such games stimulate lively lateral thinking and decision-making, providing the English teacher with plenty of opportunities for predictive and creative writing. Nevertheless they tend to have various limitations which I have found frustrating: some have very restricted vocabularies, others allow only two-word commands, and they often allow only one solution - however imaginative - for any specific dilemma. So, using the genre as a starting-point I embarked on the development (at Chelsea College) of a suite of programs which would allow children and teachers to produce their own ADVENTURE games.

ADVENTURER, as the package is called, does not involve any actual programming on the part of the users. They begin by imagining some kind of scenario, and then type in a series of locations to act as scenes for the action. They need to decide on a plot for the participants to be involved with - perhaps exploring a magical land in search of a famous wizard, or escaping from a school in which they find themselves locked during a holiday. The writers must leave around sufficient useful items for resourceful players to progress through the "plot" and to reach an ending, rather in the manner of the classic detective story. They can introduce characters other than the players (each of whom will also appear as a character in the story, so that every time the game is played the story is different). The group also need to teach the computer to recognise all the words which the players might reasonably be expected to need in order to command the computer (such as OPEN and DOOR to open doors). The computer has to be told what to do or "say" in reaction to both words and actions, so a considerable predictive feat is required of the writing group.

After some trial runs, which may be very lengthy when the original framework will be seen to need some patching-up at least, the story will be ready to be "played" by another group. Each member of the playing group will have a turn, and the format of the game is such that effective strategies involve working together: on a pitch-dark cave it's not very helpful for the only member of the group with a torch to wander off on her own.

This activity would not of course replace more conventional story-making. Some of the skills involved might overlap, and I would certainly hope that using ADVENTURER might result in a greater awareness of structure as well as excitement in writing stories, but the main value of the activitiy for me would be the possibilities it offered for constructive group discussion.

### Ronald Robot Rides Again?

English teachers unfamiliar with the possibilities of educational computing often fear that computers in English must mean programmed drill in spelling and grammar: some kind of electronic Ronald Ridout workbook. As far as the use of computers in the classroom is concerned, their only fear need be that the lure of the technology may seduce some teachers into using the microcomputer in this way. The only effective way to lessen this possibility is not by ignoring this new tool on the grounds that it can be abused, but by becoming involved in exploring more liberating applications. However, it seems to me that the real danger will come not from within schools, but from commercial software houses riding the home-computer boom. Attractively packaged drills in what are popularly perceived as "the Basics" in English will undoubtedly appeal to many parents anxious to use their latest acquisition to help their children. Ironically, such a use of the technology will fetter rather than assist the unfortunate victims, who need to learn how to control the technology, not to be controlled by it. English teachers could have a renewed battle on their hands against parental notions that English is a passive, atomistic, convergent activity. If they are perceived simply as being anti-technology their protestations may fall on deaf ears.

It would be misleading to suggest that there is already a wealth of good quality software already available for mainstream English. Apart, of course, from the mass of drill-and-practice software which passes under the title of "English" in commercial software catalogues, I have already referred to some suitable software which is just beginning to become available. But more English teachers need to become aware of the possibilities so that they can begin to rectify the situation: firstly, by creating a demand for software for which they should set the standards, and secondly by becoming involved in program design themselves.

## REFERENCES

1.  Chandler, D., The Potential of the Microcomputer in the English Classroom. *New Directions in English Teaching*, ed. Adams. Falmer Press, p. 91 (1982).

2.  Papert, S., *Mindstorms: Children, Computers and Powerful Ideas*, p. 30 Basic Books (1980).

3.  Keith, G., New Machine for Old Mechanics? in *Exploring English with Microcomputers*, ed. Chandler, CET/MEP (1983).

4.  Sharples, M., A Construction Kit for Language, *Exploring English with Microcomputers*, ed. Chandler, CET/MEP (1983).

5.  Adams, A., Why English Teachers Should Use Computers, *Exploring English with Microcomputers*, ed. Chandler, CET/MEP (1983).

6.  Jewson, J., Sheingold, K., Gearhart, M. and Berger, C., *Microcomputers in Schools: Impact on the Social Life of Elementary Classrooms*, Bank Street College of Education, New York (1981).

7.  Chandler (1982), *op.cit.*, pp. 81-83.

# COMPUTER BASED LEARNING MODULES FOR EARLY ADOLESCENCE

David Trowbridge and Alfred Bork

## Introduction

Applications of computer assisted learning in our schools seem to have potentially great educational value. In this chapter we concentrate on one aspect of computer based learning: interactive dialogues for science and mathematics instruction. We describe a project for developing computer based materials designed to assist early adolescents (twelve to fourteen years) to develop abstract reasoning skills. Interactive computer programs are being produced dealing with scientific and mathematical subjects which engage pupils in dialogues emphasizing formal thought. Examples will be presented which demonstrate how carefully designed help sequences can be used to address common problems of pupils. The learning modules make extensive use of graphics and emphasize active participation by the pupil. They run on inexpensive, standalone microcomputers.

### Feasibility of Computer Based Tutorials

Evidence from both education and computer technology suggests that the implementation of effective tutorial dialogues is now feasible on small standalone machines. We note first of all that pupils display great commonality in the processes whereby they learn new material. Often they go through the same steps and encounter the same pitfalls along the way. Experienced teachers in every field share the observation that pupils repeatedly understand important concepts in the same way, and predictably display certain preconceptions which are impediments to learning the crucial ideas of that field (1,2,3,4,5). In developing educational materials we must both capitalize on the similarities and provide for the individual differences among pupils. Computer based materials provide a way to do this.

Suitably programmed, microcomputers can mimic the alertness of a skilled tutor. They are uniquely capable of analyzing pupil input and branching accordingly. They can provide reinforcement, carefully phrased questions or extensive help sequences. Microcomputer graphics is now reaching a stage where high quality drawings and animation are possible.

## Examples of Dialogues Involving Ratio Reasoning

### I.   Density

The concept of density involves reasoning with the ratio of mass to volume. Ratio reasoning is widely recognized as one component of formal thought. It is a skill which is prerequisite to understanding many of the concepts which are part of the middle school science and mathematics curriculum.

We will describe briefly a computer dialogue that deals with this concept. The dialogue has three parts, emphasizing respectively the concepts of mass, volume and density. To give continuity and motivation to the target age pupils, the dialogue is embedded in a fanciful story line involving a search for "energy-producing crystals". The energy producing crystals are characterized as consisting of some unique material. The key to the solution of the puzzle lies in the fact that among several candidates, three particular crystals have the same density. When the inference is made that the ones with the same density consist of the same material, a test is performed to determine whether indeed they produce energy when placed together.

The exercise involves a variety of experimental investigations conducted by pupils as if they were actually in a laboratory provided with a balance, a graduated cylinder and a number of other devices for measuring the physical properties of crystals. For instance, in the first activity pupils are presented with pictures of a magnet and a collection of crystals. Using directional arrow keys on the keyboard, they move the magnet near the crystals to find out whether each crystal is attracted to it. They are provided with a picture of an equal arm balance and a set of standard weights which they use to determine the mass of each crystal. Using very simple animation, we simulate the operations of placing the object to be weighed on one pan of the balance and placing a number of standard masses on the other pan until a pointer indicates that the pans are in balance.

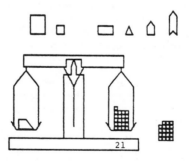

Figure I:  Simulated measurement of mass

In the investigations of both magnetic attraction and mass, the pupil is actually performing experiments to obtain data. At the end of the first activity, the pupil is introduced to the distinction between intensive and extrinsic properties. Magnetism is characteristic of material composition, and independent of the size of the sample; hence, magnetism is called an intrinsic property. Mass on the other hand depends on the size of the sample and is called extrinsic.

The second activity involved investigations of shape and volume, carried out in the same manner. Two approaches to the concept of volume are taken. The first involves building a stack of unit cubes which approximates in size and shape the crystal to be measured, and then counting the cubes in the stack.

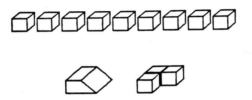

**Figure 2: Measurement of volume by counting cubes**

The second involves a graduated cylinder with water. Initially, the cylinder is calibrated by placing unit cubes in the water and recording the water level after each addition. Then, the volume of each crystal is measured by water displacement.

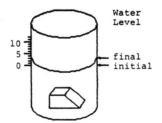

**Figure 3: Measurement of volume by water displacement**

The objective of the third activity is for the pupil to be able to calculate density from mass and volume numbers, and to interpret the result of dividing mass by volume as the number of kilograms contained in each one litre of the material. There are a number of branch points at various places in the activity on density, and each branch has subsequent remedial activities for the pupil.

As teachers, we frequently encounter pupils who have learned rules of division and are able to divide one interger into another, but in real world problems involving division are often either unable to set up the problem correctly, or unable to interpret their result. Our goal in teaching the concept of density goes beyond having pupils memorize the formula D = M/V. We want the pupil to be able to interpret the result of dividing mass by volume as well. That is, the pupil should understand density as the mass contained in each one unit of volume in the object.

The computer dialogue on density contains several branch points at which the pupil's understanding is assessed. If necessary, the program routes the pupil through a brief tutorial sequence. One such sequence involves a hypothetical instrument called a "laser knife". The function of the laser knife is to extract a unit cube of material from a selected crystal. The unit cube is then weighed on a balance to determine the density number directly. This demonstrates one of the great strengths of experiments using computer graphics: the experimental tools can be designed for optimal pedagogical impact without regard to any of the "messy" effects inherent in an actual laboratory equipment. The laser knife extracts a precise unit cube quickly, cleanly, and effortlessly.

The help sequence establishes a connection between the equivalent processes of obtaining density directly by weighing a unit cube, and computing density by dividing total mass by total volume. This step too is facilitated by graphics in which the crystal is broken into several unit cubes and then units of mass are evenly distributed to each of the unit cubes. Thus the mathematical process of dividing by a volume number is presented as a physical process of breaking up an object into a number of pieces of unit volume.

We believe that development of the formal skill of reasoning with ratios in the context of density is encouraged by concrete experiences in the same context. Thus, while the goal of this dialogue is to develop the pupil's facility with mass/volume ratios, the approach to that goal involves a manipulative task requiring only concrete reasoning.


## 2.  Speed

Another dialogue we are developing in this same group concerns the concept of speed. Once again, this concept involves a ratio; fostering understanding of this ratio is the goal of this dialogue.

Without formal reasoning skills a child is generally capable of judging (using concrete reasoning) which of two objects is faster when the motions are at least partly simultaneous (6). That is, when two objects travelling along parallel paths start and stop at the same instant, the child has no difficulty comparing speeds on the basis of the distances travelled by the objects. Similarly, when the distances travelled are the same but either the starting times or ending times are non-simultaneous then the child may compare speeds on the basis of the time required to traverse equal distances.

However, when both displacements and time intervals differ, or when the motions are entirely non-simultaneous, concrete reasoning is no longer satisfactory for comparing speeds. Instead, the child must construct some kind of ratio (either distance travelled for each unit of time, or time required for each unit of distance) to make a successful comparison. According to Piaget, this is a component of formal thought.

In the computer dialogue on speed, the pupil is provided with an experimental arrangement which simulates the rectilinear motions of two balls travelling along parallel paths. Some of the motions are under user control, while others are demonstrated by the program for the purpose of asking the pupil to compare two motions.

Launchers

**Figure 4: Animation for comparison of uniform motions**

In the beginning exploratory activity, a black ball is controlled by the program and a while ball is controlled by the pupil. A device resembling the launcher on a pinball machine has a "spring" which can be "stretched" using simple key press commands (Figure 4). Upon a launch command, a ball moves across the screen at a constant speed which depends upon the initial extension of the spring launcher. Tasks are presented to the pupil such as, "make the white ball go faster than the black ball and pass it", or "make the white ball start behind, stay behind, but travel with a speed greater than the black ball".

The next two activities involve demonstrations of two balls which travel equal distances in unequal terms or take equal times to travel unequal distances. Pupils are asked, "Was the speed of the white ball greater than, less than or the same speed of the black ball?" Each example provides a situation in which the concepts of position and speed must be discriminated (for example, the distinction between being ahead and travelling faster).

Sometimes, the motion of the balls is hidden under two tunnels except at the endpoints so that comparisons of speed must be made in terms of the variables of distance and time rather than on the visual phenomena of catching up, overtaking or falling behind (Figure 5).

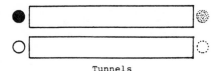

Tunnels

**Figure 5: Comparison of motions using tunnels**

In the fourth activity, the ratio concept is introduced. If the pupil has any difficulty making comparisons of small whole number ratios, help sequences are provided. In one case, the pupil is provided with the option of analyzing the motion of each ball by measuring directly how far it moves in one second. That is, by repeating to launch a ball at the same speed each time (from a spring of constant extension), the pupil may choose to view the path of the ball executed during a unit time interval. In this way a connection is established between the mathematical operation of dividing a distance by a time interval and the operation of measuring the path directly which corresponds to a unit time. Computer animation provides a simple way of performing these experiments and leaving a visual record of the motion.

Additional help sequences are provided for pupils who still have difficulty with the idea of dividing. For example, an analogy is presented between dividing a line segment into a number of equal pieces and dividing a quantity of money equally among friends.

**Other Dialogues Involving Formal Reasoning**

Other dialogues currently under development to aid formal reasoning treat some other topics which are relevant to middle school science and mathematics programmes: 7 classification of triangles, the concept of area, mathematical estimation, number relations and graphing. Each emphasizes one or more reasoning skills which are characteristic of formal thought. In addition to the dialogues involving reasoning with ratio and proportion, we are developing materials for control of variables, hypothetical reasoning and inductive reasoning.

Each dialogue is written as a Module composed of from three to six separate activities. Each activity takes the pupil between five and fifteen minutes to complete. Pupils may perform the activities on different days if they choose. The activities build on one another, beginning with exploratory exercises, continuing with sections that introduce key concepts, and concluding with an activity requiring application of the concepts to some slightly new situation.

We have not as yet undertaken a programme for evaluation of

144

the effectiveness of these materials. However, informal experience suggests that these interactive dialogues do serve the function of engaging pupils in interesting, thought provoking experiments from which they gain valuable practice in scientific reasoning. The dialogues are, first and foremost interactive in nature, requiring frequent input from the learner and diverse branching opportunities for guidance through appropriate help sequences. The modules should prove useful in middle school classrooms to serve functions of both enrichment and remedial help. The interactive nature of the dialogue makes them ideal for individualized instruction.

## Summary

We have attempted to demonstrate that computer based educational materials can provide useful tutorial assistance to young adolescent pupils. An examination of the common conceptual problems and troubles with scientific reasoning of pupils at this age suggests that automated dialogues overcome these difficulties. We have described two examples of programs which attempt to do this. Loth have been concerned with the reasoning which underlies the understanding of two important physical concepts: density and speed.

## REFERENCES

1.   diSessa, A.A., Unlearning Aristotelian Physics: A Study of Knowledge Based Learning, Unpublished manuscript, Division for Study and Research in Education, Massachussetts Institute of Technology (September, 1980).

2.   Hawkins, D., Critical Barriers to Science Learning, *Outlook*, Issue no. 29, Mountain View Centre for Environmental Education, University of Colorado, Boulder (1978).

3.   McCloskey, M., Carramazza, A. and Green, B., Curvilinear Motion in the Absence of External Forces: Naive Beliefs About the Motion of Objects, *Science, 210*, 1139-41 (1980).

4.   Trowbridge, D.E. and McDermott, L.C., Investigation of Student Understanding of the Concept of Velocity in One Dimension, *American Journal of Physics, 48*, 1020-28 (1980).

5.   Trowbridge, D.A. and McDermott, L.C., Investigation of Student Understanding of the Concept of Acceleration in One Dimension, *American Journal of Physics, 49*, 242-53 (1981).

**145**

6.    Piaget, J., *The Child's Conception of Movement and Speed*, Ballantine Books, New York (1970).

7.    Trowbridge, D.E. and Bork, A., A Computer Based Dialog for Developing Mathematical Reasoning of Young Adolescents, Proceedings of the National Educational Computing Conference, Denton, Texas, U.S.A. (June, 1981).

# COMPUTERS AND SECOND LANGUAGE LEARNING

Gareth Roberts

Modern linguists are somewhat traditional in their outlook and many are wary of technological advances. Indeed there can be a general mistrust of machinery which always seems to break down or not to perform to specification. Anyway, modern language teachers have more important things to worry them such as the apparent lack of interest in their subject and the current methodological tussles between traditionalists and modernists. Furthermore, like many other teachers, they see that computers are in short supply in school, not generally available to them or their classes, seem to be more suited to individual rather than class use and need considerable effort to understand and manipulate.

Perhaps, however, the real reason for the apparent lack of interest in CALL (Computer Assisted Language Learning) is that modern linguists feel that computers are not *appropriate* to language teaching. It is argued that computers are not "sociable beings" whereas language is concerned with people interacting with each other rather than people interacting with machines (I). It is thought that linguistic contact between people makes it easier to "generalise" to real-life situations outside the classroom. Modern teaching stresses the teaching of the "spoken" language and at the moment there seem to be limits to computer speech production and reception so that there is heavy scepticism towards those who advocate CALL and there is a mistrust of self-professed "experts" in this field. In spite of this opposition there are a growing number of language teachers who are beginning to realise that the computer can perhaps be an useful aid in language teaching and who wish to be informed of the teaching possibilities of computers. It is to these people that this article is addressed. It is meant to give a balanced account of such possibilities, an account of some of the work done in the field and an indication of the potential of CALL.

## Useful Computer Characteristics

### The Storage of Data

Language is concerned with words and sentences and the computer is capable of alphanumeric storage of information. An ability to deal with strings of characters is a pre-requisite for the teaching of languages. It might well be true that the storage of information could be made more easily on paper or in a book but the computer has the ability to search for information and check its accuracy compared with the user's requirements. For example, if one enters the infinitive of a German strong verb the computer will search for this verb and if it is found it will display all relevant information concerning the forms for the different tenses and moods (2). This can save time and ensure that the user does not obtain the incorrect answer. It is wrong to assume that most pupils can use books correctly. There is no guarantee that a pupil is on the correct page, never mind the correct line, but the computer can select the correct information and present it at the correct time. Furthermore the computer can be made to display the information for a certain length of time only. We shall return to this feature when considering the teaching of reading and merely note in passing that simple electronic dictionaries which are really "one to one" phrase books are now available for travellers and are suitable for formulaic utterances only.

*String Handling*

In language teaching it is the string-handling facilities of the computer that can be most useful. We find, for example in school text-books that it is usual to give the future tense in full of only one French verb as the future endings of all verbs are regular. The pupil is then expected to generalise the information to other verbs. Some pupils succeed in doing this, but others certainly fail. A computer program can work out the forms economically so that the future tense of any verb can be stated in full.

*Interactive Reaction with the User*

It is the interaction between pupil and computer that makes it such an useful teaching tool. The pupil is required to respond to stimuli from the computer. The stimuli can be of different kinds, for example, translating a word or sentence, choosing one of a multiple choice of answers to questions, giving a foreign language word or phrase, choosing a correct sequence of letters or numbers or indicating that he or she wishes to continue or revise previous responses, or that he or she requires help of some sort. This makes the computer an individual teaching machine worthy of serious consideration.

*Branches and Loops*

The interactive element of computer teaching is greatly strengthened by the computer's ability to repeat in full or in part any information or display. Thus the rate of progress can be tailored to the individual pupil's requirements. This repetition of material is most important as *consolidation* of the work learnt is vital. In addition as learners differ in their rate of comprehension and need different types and degrees of help the branching abilities of computers are useful; for example, it is possible to give only to those children who need it, grammatical information which can be as sparse or as detailed as the learner requires.

## Computer Graphics and Animation

Computer graphics means the drawing of pictures or symbols by the computer. Modern linguists have been slow to use this facility, and as it requires more programming expertise and time this is perhaps understandable. However, manufacturers are continually improving the facility and this will ensure that their use will become easier and more widespread. What follows is a brief outline of the possible uses of graphics. Experience seems to suggest that people tire easily with text and that a type of word-blindness can occur. The traditional screen menu can perhaps be replaced with pictures and symbols because these would be more effective from the perceptual point of view. A single picture can give more information than a long verbal description. Adventure games are now appearing with pictures of caves and dungeons rather than descriptions in words.

In language teaching a certain amount of reality needs to be maintained and a picture can form a link between the learner and the work he is doing. For example he can relate to a picture of a cafe or of an airport and can imagine himself in that situation. Pictures themselves can provide interest because they lend variety to the program. It is useful if a program is "top and tailed" with a visual which can give unity to the whole activity. A picture at the beginning arouses interest and a picture at the end awakens interest in running the program again.

The teaching of any subject can involve the presentation of abstract concepts and if these concepts can be explained in visual terms then perhaps they will be understood better. For example the concept of gender can be represented by the picture of a man and woman. "Singular" can be represented by one person and "plural" by more than one. Sometimes one does not wish to explain what is happening and one can avoid any explanation merely by illustrating. For example the author has a program where the past participles of verbs are brought in by a helicopter; no explanation is given of the term but its location and function as part of the verb is made clear.

Visuals can clearly indicate when one part of a program is over and another is beginning - this is done by means of "wipes and fades" also by "scrolls". This gives the pupil a recovery time and a break until the next task. Visuals can have a beneficial psychological effect, for example by the use of a favourite cartoon character to introduce work or by means of a pleasant picture. An example of this is a Texas Instruments Grammar Program which in part of the program uses a picture of a train and signals with various windows for words. The picture is not really relevant to the material but is pleasant to look at for a young child and perhaps sweetens the pill of grammar!

In certain language teaching situations it is impossible to use the native tongue to give instructions. This happens very often in the teaching of English as a second language when children from different linguistic backgrounds may be found in the same class. If one uses a picture of an eraser to indicate "correct an error", or the picture of a pencil for "write in your answer", a picture of an eye for "look" and so on one can begin to communicate visually.

Pictures can be used without language to illustrate objects, actions, situations, colours, shapes, sizes and also the relationship between different objects (bigger than, older than) and this can lead to a host of exercises based on pictures - question and answer, substitution, multiple choice and so on.

Pictures can also be the *symbols* of certain linguistic connotations, so that the presentation of a symbol always recalls a whole series of procedures to be carried out by the pupil through an association of ideas. A picture of a book might indicate a procedure such as "Look up the form in your dictionary", or "write the form correctly in your book" or "learn the form".

Animation can be particularly effective since it attracts the eye and motivates interest. Animation may be under computer control and may consist merely of the building up of parts of a picture for example a house with all the rooms or it can consist of actual movements such as walking or running whereby moving figures can be used to test verbs, direction and movement.

Of equal interest is animation under user control, the basis of all arcade games which involve the learner in active manipulation. This provides a high degree of motivation. Movement under user control could be incorporated into a language teaching program. For example, it could be used with the plan of a town, with the learner being required to follow directions to a certain location.

## Computer Sound

Sound effects are much used in computer games but can also serve an useful teaching purpose. Typical uses might be as follows. A sound effect can acknowledge that the computer has received an answer or could function as a reward. A variety of such rewards could be given in a program. Furthermore a sound effect can be the symbol for a certain character, situation or mood. A sound effect can be used to indicate a catastrophe such as a crashing car or a boat sinking. It can also act as a prompt if an answer is a long time in coming or if the learner is required to be particularly attentive. A nasty sound can also be the same as a reprimand for an incorrect answer. Sound effects can also add realism for linguistic situations for example train sounds, whistles etc.

It is with care that one mentions computer music since many

pupils are tired of the theme music as an introduction to language units. Nevertheless music can contribute to computer-based programs. The music can serve as a reprimand for an error and also act as a mood introducer. It can act as a situation introducer such as "The Orient Express" theme for travel. The music can also serve as a musical link between two parts of a program and corresponds to the visual link mentioned previously. Musical cues also find a direct use in language teaching - countries or nationalities can be identified by national anthems or occupations by appropriate tunes.

The computer can synthesise speech and systems are available to do so. These involve synthesising language from a total of 60 "phonemes". Any word or phrase can be built in this way but until now the sound has been very "Dalek" like. Synthesised speech can be incorporated directly into a program and repeated at will. There is however, a limit to the authenticity of such speech reproduction at the moment - although there is great commercial, military and educational pressure for improvement. Allophonic systems are being developed which allow intonation patterns and a certain amount of individual voice difference. However, the rate of technological development in this field is such that we should be thinking more in terms of working out worthwhile teaching schemes incorporating the current technology rather than follow day to day technological advances.

A more practical approach at the present time is the use of the synchronisation of tape-recorded speech with the recorder under computer control. This system is used in the Atari conversational language series. The main disadvantage of this system is that the tape cannot be returned for replay of a sentence without disturbing the synchronisation and thus the program has to be linear - at least from the point of view of the presentation of the sound. On the other hand the technique is effective, allows the use of different voices and is relatively simple.

**The Teaching of Grammar**

Many of the language teaching programs produced so far have been grammar-based. This might reflect the current requirements of public examinations of the tradition in which many teachers have been brought up or it could be related to the particular ease with which the computer is able to store and process data according to fixed rules.

In the teaching of grammar the computer can (a) act as the teacher of rules (b) supply a corpus of well-formed utterances from which the learner should be able to generalize his own rules and (c) calculate the correct grammatical form for the pupil whenever necessary (3). First the computer states the grammatical rule and from the pupil's response to questions, checks whether certain items have been understood. If not the learner is referred to a remedial branch in the program. The main program then illustrates the rule from items in its data store and initiates a test procedure to ensure that the

**151**

material has been learnt or if there is a need for the pupil to be taken back to relearn the rule. By means of testing procedures it is possible for the program to decide which approach to take with pupils-rule learning, rule illustration or "calculator" function. Illustrations and examples are given in reference (3).

## A Communicative Approach

At least one commercially available program (4) follows the "communicative" approach to language teaching and the following remarks are based on an assessment of the material. It is an audio-active course with the cassette recorder controlled by the computer supplying the speech. The program follows the following set of procedures.

(a)    *A statement of aims* is provided for each unit - this is an important psychological ploy in communicative teaching. The learner is told what he is about to learn and its practical relevance is made explicit.

(b)    *A look and listen* section follows which displays German language text on the screen with English translation following each sentence. The tape recorder is switched on and the German sentence is stated sometimes with accompanying graphics.

(c)    *Look, listen and repeat.* This section has the same sentences on screen as in "look and listen" but without the English translation. The voice states the sentence and "Repeat" flashes on the screen with a spaced gap for the learner to reply. The learner repeats the sentence but of course the computer cannot check the pronunciation and the intervention of a teacher is useful at this stage. The "look, listen and repeat" section of the program can be repeated but the tape cannot be rerun and the voice cannot be repeated.

(d)    *Think, choose and repeat* is an aural comprehension exercise. A voice asks a question or makes a statement and the learner is given a choice of two responses. The program continues only when the correct response is given, in which case the correct response is given in both voice and visual form.

(e)    *Quick repeat.* This section is used to introduce additional vocabulary with an illustration sometimes accompanying the written word. The new vocabulary is reinforced by the voice on the tape.

(f)    *Situational role playing.* A picture of the situation (e.g. party, airport) is provided and instructions given such as "Take the part of the man in this scene, ask the lady what her name is". The computer follows any response with the correct words on the screen and on tape. The computer, as yet, has no means of checking pronunciation but in this respect it is no different from conventional cassette-based "teach yourself" courses. Where the computer gains considerably

**152**

over cassette courses is the continuous prompting and guidance that it gives.

(g)  *Extension exercises.*  These are reading exercises with the extended vocabulary without an oral component.

*Extended aural comprehension.*  These are either short extracts from different situations (e.g., bank, petrol-station etc.) or more lengthy situation (20-30 seconds).  Comprehension is tested by means of multiple-choice questions.

In spite of some weakness the course is a well-produced and worthy "first generation" Computer Assisted Language Learning course in which the computer is used for both initial learning and consolidation.

## The Teaching of Reading

Reading in this context means the intensive reading demanded for examination purposes by many examination boards at CSE, O and A level.  The purpose of the computer assisted learning technique is to instill into the candidates reading and behavioural patterns which will be automatic when faced with a reading passage under examination conditions.  The following is a typical procedure.

a)  *Initial familiarization*  The computer displays each numbered sentence of the passage one by one accompanied perhaps by a synchronised sound track.  The timing of the appearance of the sentences on the screen corresponds to the normal reading speed. This could be repeated say three times so that the pupil has to look at the passage sentence by sentence and listen to the sound.

b)  *Familiarization*  Each sentence in the passage is presented on the screen with the following menu (i) A translation of the sentence to check comprehension. (ii) A list of pronunciation hints with each sentence, for example nasals or silent nasals.  (iii)  With each sentence a graphical representation of the intonation pattern. (iv) An option to blank out unpronounced letters and show liaisons.

c)  *Repetition*  The computer displays the sentence word by word at normal reading speed with a synchronised reading of the sentence. This gives the pupil a model to imitate and to correlate the spoken and written form of the sentence.

d)  *Correction*  The synchronised sound track of the sentence is provided once more.  This allows the pupil to self-correct what he has just said.

e)  *Paragraph consolidation.*  At the end of the paragraph the whole paragraph can be displayed and a recording played.  This provides a model of the complete paragraph which can then be read aloud.

f)    *Paragraph correction*  A recording of the whole paragraph is played again to allow the pupil to correct any errors and imitate the recording.  Finally the whole passage is displayed sentence by sentence at normal reading speed with the pupil required to read this under examination conditions without further help.

This sequence is not novel but typical of what a teacher might do to teach pupils how to read a passage of a foreign language.  The computer can control the sequence of events and releases the teacher to circulate among pupils to give them extra help or extra confidence. This technique is for individual work but could function with a small group.

**The Teaching of Vocabulary**

Two computer facilities make it useful for the teaching of vocabulary, namely the fact that the computer can compare an answer typed in with data it holds, and also repeat vocabulary items until acquired by the learner **(5).**   The following illustrates a vocabulary teaching program.

1)    *Introduction.* List the words to be learnt with their meanings. There should not be too many (perhaps 10-20). Relate the vocabulary to the pupil's text-book or other print source.

2)    *Familiarisation.*  Where possible words should be in the same linguistic context (e.g. parts of the car, clothes) and a composite picture presented.   Each element is taken in turn and its pronunciation stated clearly with synchronised speech.   Time is allowed for repetition by the pupil and the spelling of the word displayed with the picture or with the English translation.

3)    *Passive acquisition.*  Take a sequence of about five elements together.  A picture and the spelling of each word is displayed and the pupils are required to match them up correctly.

4)    *Active acquisition.*  This usually means acquisition of the spelling and can be assisted by asking the pupils to type out the word which they see flashed momentarily on the screen.   With each repetition the time the word remains on the screen can be reduced until finally the pupils have to spell the word without seeing the word.

5)    *Consolidation.*  The word is to be used correctly in a grammatical context by filling in the blanks in sentences.

Rewards are extremely important in this type of program. Praise is required for every correct answer and an increased reward for a sequence of correct answers. It is a good idea to have a "supreme" reward for having all answers correct.

## Rewards and Software Psychology

Modern linguists need to reinforce pupil's correct answers much more than in many other subjects because the work itself often does not bring its own reward, except perhaps for the more able pupils. Less able pupils need constant encouragement and help and this is part of the teacher's stock in trade. The pupils must be actively motivated to participate. One of the fundamental appeals of computers is that they are innately fascinating to many people. Nevertheless techniques need to be developed to actively reward pupils.

The most obvious reward is verbal. This is very easy to arrange and is often incorporated in the most unsophisticated programs. Verbal praise can be made more attractive by making it appear in large and/or coloured letters, enhanced by wipes and fades so that the whole effect is of a pleasant visual experience.

The use of a *score* is well-established in computer games. Ideally the task should be difficult enough so that satisfaction is obtained but without it being so difficult that the learner is discouraged. Another reward which can be used is *time on a game*. This could be a simple game at the end of a program, access to which is allowed only as a reward. Ideally this game should also be a language game. As many children are hooked on computer games this could be a worthwhile reward. An *attainable goal* such as the winning of a horse race or scoring a goal or seeing a rocket build up and taking off gives a sense of satisfaction to the learner (6). Another possibility is an *unpredictable reward* (e.g., a little man taking off his hat, bowing and applauding). *Variety* of reward is as essential as a variety of language presentation.

## Language Games

### Computer language games

Language games have now become respectable and computer versions of some of those in use are either available or can be made. Word games are always popular and computer versions of "Hangman" complete with sound, animation and colour graphics are available. The author has also used a variety called "Executioner" (7) where the learner must guess the word and for every wrong letter the guillotine falls down a step. After eight failures a head rolls as the guillotine finishes its journey and the correct answer given. The popular computer magazines are an excellent source of potential games, many of which can be adapted for educational purposes.

### Computer language simulation games

Computers can provide simulations of real language situations. Involvement in a game can allow the learner to lose some of his inhibitions and if the game uses language then language learning can take place. Computer adventure games often involve competing against other players, making or losing money, or reaching a goal and overcoming difficulties on the way. Sometimes there is also a race against time. Many adventure games make heavy demands on the imagination with dungeons and castles and unreal places. Also the characters tend to be unreal, for example monsters, giants and goblins.

Language games, however, need to be realistic. The locations and objects in the game must be practical, for example cafes and groceries and items of food rather than buried treasure. The characters should also be authentic such as policemen, passers-by and officials. Furthermore the situations must be realistic enough for the learner to feel a personal involvement in the game. The games should also involve a graphical representation of the situation to enhance the authenticity and to provide a visual stimulus.

An element of decision making is often present in adventure games and this can also be present in language situation simulations. For example a pupil can be asked to check on comprehension or alternatively the program can place the learner in a situation in which he might well find himself for example being lost. Does he ask a passer-by, keep on searching or buy a map? The learner could also be given role playing conversational tasks to complete.

The computer lacks the human authenticity of language use but nevertheless can develop an appreciation of real language situations and develop the child's imagination and linguistic ability.

## REFERENCES

1. Govier, H., Primary Language Development, *Acorn User*, 45, (May 1983).

2. 2x81 German Language System, Program 5, Precision Software Engineers, Newark.

3. Roberts, G.W., The Use of Microcomputers for the Teaching of Modern Languages, *The British Journal of Language Teaching*, *19*, 125 (1981).

4. Conversational French, German, Spanish, Italian, Atari International.

5. Hargreaves, J., French Vocabulary Program for the BBC microcomputer.

6. French Countdown, AVC, Birmingham.

7. Toland, P., Execution, *ZX Computing*, 92, (December 1982).

8. Davies, G. and Higgins, J., Computers, Language & Learning, *Information Guide 22*, CILT, London.

# MICROELECTRONICS IN SCHOOLS AND COLLEGES

Graham Bevis

M.E.P., the Microelectronics in Education Programme, is an unprecedented initiative in the history of our education system. It was conceived by James Callaghan, Labour Prime Minister, during the first years of "silicon chip" fever when TV programmes, such as "Now the chips are down", highlighted the implications of this technology for our whole way of life. M.E.P. is unprecedented in that it is an initiative with a wide ranging brief covering many activities such as curriculum development, teacher training; consulting with Industry, Higher Education and Examination Boards to seek support and consensus for the changes in the curriculum which are likely to follow the Programme's activity. The range of potential influence in Education of "microelectronics", which means different things to different people, is evident in the organisation of the M.E.P. The activity is divided into five domains; Computer Based Learning, the Computer as an Instrument, Communication and Information Studies, Special Education, Electronics and Control Technology (which is the subject of this paper).

The major statement of the M.E.P. strategy conceived by Richard Fothergill, the Programme Director, reads:

"The aim of the Programme is to help schools to prepare children for life in a society in which devices and systems based on microelectronics are commonplace and pervasive. These technologies are likely to alter the relationships between one individual and another and between individuals and their work; and people will need to be aware that the speed of change is accelerating and that their future careers may well include many retraining stages as they adjust to new technological developments."

The all pervasive nature of Microelectronics Technology itself provides a justification for the inclusion of some "New Technology" study as part of the curriculum of all pupils; particularly as this pervasiveness will become increasingly significant in its influence on our fortunes and way of life. It would therefore, seem sensible that

**157**

with our democratic society, the population as a whole should have some insight into the principles of the New Technology in order to perceive its capability, its benefits and dangers. They should then be able to influence the political decisions which determine the way in which the technology develops and is applied.

To emphasize the pervasive aspect the following table catalogues some of the day to day activities which have become transformed by microtechnology in what amounts to two decades of rapid advance; advances which themselves provide the basis for further progress.

## Exponential Technology

| | |
|---|---|
| Timekeeping | Sundial - Digital systems and sequence control |
| Entertainment | Stones - Video chess<br>Percussion - Synthesisers |
| Washing | Stones/Rivers - Programmed washing machine |
| Food | Charcoal - Microwave - Remote programmable cookers |
| Communications | Signal fires - Satelite links<br>Towncrier - Ceefax, Oracle, Prestel, System X |
| Calculation | Tally sticks - Napier's bones - Microcomputers |
| Medicine | Herbal remedies - Thermometers -EEG - Scanners - Computer aided diagnosis |
| Transport | Walking - digitally controlled cars - space |
| Warfare | Tooth and claw - computerised overkill |
| Education | Mother's knee - Computer assisted learning - Databases - video disc |
| Weather forecasting | Folklore - Satellites, scanning and communication, computers |
| Information Storage | Cave walls - Microfilm - Government Computers - video disk |
| Farming | Hand and hoe - computerised milking parlour and digital tractors |

The table is headed "Exponential Technology" because each step forward increases the base for the next step and consequently its potential magnitude.

It must be emphasised that the power of New Technology is not due to some highly complicated new discovery. In fact the rapid advance is due to a coming together of many separate fields of human achievement united by the common medium of semiconductor technology utilising digital techniques. The elements of even sophisticated digital systems depend on the use of many simple principles. The cleverness arises from the way these principles have been brought together. There is no great mystery or complication, a sensible appreciation of New Technology is not reserved for a super intelligent elite. On the contrary teachers are finding that younger pupils and less able pupils assimulate these new ideas very readily and confidently, particularly when the study is practically based, does not depend on prior knowledge for success and is interactive at a very personal level.

The underlying principles of New Technology are simple and an appreciation of these enables an understanding of a very wide range of products and systems embodying their application. The fields of human knowledge and enterprise, which have been brought together as Information Technology, are those of information storage (previously largely paper based), information processing (previously inhibited by the limited accessibility of paper based information) and information communication (previously limited by the low volume flow rate enabled by old technologies). Most significantly these capabilities have enabled "Control Technology", recognisable in "Robotics", to extend the usefulness of the machine technology of the industrial revolution to control large forces and large power more effectively.

In politics and education there is much confusion about the term "microelectronics", and all too often the word is commuted to microprocessor which in turn becomes microcomputer. The resulting confusion is that Information Technology is largely about computers. Computer Studies as a subject is often regarded as an education in "New Technology". Computers are part of new technology but the digital processor itself appears in many more guises than the one typified by a keyboard and a VDU. Computer Studies, as currently taught in schools, plays only a part in developing an appreciation of the principles and implications of new technology.

### The M.E.P. Electronics and Control Technology Domain

Studies of basic electronics, microelectronics and the use of programmed electronic devices as *controllers* have become part of the syllabus of many new and established school courses: This includes syllabuses in which the major study is electronics, e.g., the many new 'O' and 'A' level syllabuses entitled Electronics, Electricity and Electronics, Electronic Systems etc. and subjects in which electronics is part of the study, e.g. Control Technology, Modular Technology, Craft Design Technology, Engineering Science, Physics and some Computer Studies courses.

Many schools, fortunate to have enlightened headteachers and supportive LEAs, have already introduced new elements about Information Technology into the general curriculum, particularly into the 11-13 years age range and the sixth form. Since these approaches to "Technology Awareness" depend on the expertise, enthusiasm and initiative of individual groups many approaches may be identified but increasingly certain essential elements are common to all schemes. Significantly most if not all include a practical study of Electronic Systems "black box" style. An encouraging point of general agreement is that some form of technology awareness tailored to the needs and abilities of particular pupil groups is a fundamental part of education and is not confined to the top 20% ability range. This is not to deny the importance of the many new subject examination syllabuses which are being enthusiastically taken up by the pupils fortunate enough to be given this opportunity. As a nation we need the means to identify those pupils who have the ability to contribute to a microtechnology orientated world and to provide a vehicle to encourage and enable them to develop their potential to become creative engineers and technicians. The rapid uptake of these courses owes much to the exciting and motivating nature of the subject matter but also relates to the demand by pupils for study which is identifiably relevant.

Secondary schools which incorporate a technology awareness course for all pupils in the 11-14 range and provide specialist examination courses to follow are serving both the basic educational needs of their pupils and the need of an industrial economy for talented, creative technologists and engineering. Schools should, in these times of unemployment, also consider whether the education their pupils are given is that best fitted to make the pupils employable or alternatively to be better able to usefully occupy their non-working leisure time. Study which encourages creativity, initiative, self determination, serves both of these requirements.

The M.E.P. Electronics and Control Technology domain is concerned with INSET (in-service education for teachers) which will enable teachers to develop the necessary expertise to teach the current electronics component of the many examined and non-examined courses which include this subject. Parallel to this and frequently as part of these basic courses measures will be taken to extend this minimum expertise into the implications of current and potential new applications of microelectronic technology to all aspects of the world of life and work. Despite assertions to the contrary it is teachers who ultimately influence the content and philosophy of teaching syllabuses as well as obviously determining the day to day classroom emphasis. It is therefore essential that they develop an expert overview to influence this area of the curriculum so that it keeps pace with educational objectives which are pertinent to our changing environment. Teachers should be able to relate the concepts taught as part of basic and examinable syllabuses to their current applications as part of their normal teaching programme. Teaching has long been dominated by the theme that "we only have time to teach what will be examined". Examination syllabuses take at least five years to change or to become established and ensuring that the classroom lessons in technological subjects are obviously relevant and valid for pupils requires that teachers are able to relate the subject beyond any limits of stated syllabuses. The emphasis of teaching syllabuses must be on basic principles and techniques, the understanding of which should be developed to the point where these concepts may be related to new developments and others not the subject of specialist syllabus study.

## Approaches to Electronics Teaching, Systems vs Analysis

Early examination courses often pioneered and taught by Physics teachers tended to introduce microelectronics from the base of a study of electricity and electronics. Such a study begins with an introduction to electrical theory of very simple discrete electrical and electronic devices and then slowly proceeds to the operation of circuits. The student is introduced to all the steps in establishing the principles of why and how a particular electrical circuit operates. This approach tends to be difficult, uninteresting and highly analytical and because of constraints of time, does not proceed far enough to enable the student to develop any real awareness of the capability and potential application of microelectronic technology. A completely different approach termed "the systems approach" treats microelectronics as a subject which utilises functional "black boxes" which may be assembled together into systems to perform particular operations as the solution to a problem. To produce this assembly of "black boxes" requires a knowledge and understanding of the function of elements and procedures for interconnecting or interfacing them but does not require any knowledge of the internal operations of the "black box" elements. This means that students are able to work with a wide range of functional elements which assembled together produce systems of considerable versatility and power. This approach has many far reaching consequences in educational terms. Firstly it does not require a basis of scientific knowledge for pupils to be involved in real problem solving, design based activity. This also means of course that teaching about microtechnology using a "black box" approach can be undertaken by any teacher willing to learn a new discipline. It is not the sole province of the physicist, mathematician or craft design and technology teacher. Their ways of thinking are helpful to such teaching but their specialist basic knowledge is largely irrelevant.

The motivation factor of this medium of learning is far reaching in its consequences. Very able pupils are not constrained by the limitations of the syllabus or the classroom routine. They are free to develop their intellect by exploring possibilities which are limited only by the constraints of the hardware materials available. These limits need not be significantly constrictive because even highly sophisticated microelectronic devices are, in the raw state, very inexpensive. At the other end of the ability range pupils branded as academically less able are found to enjoy their work in designing, assembling and testing simple systems so much that their achievement resulting from the motivation enabled by an interactive

**161**

learning activity is quite unprecedented by their previous achievements in purely academic studies.

**'A' Level Electronic Systems**

The general "systems" approach is embodied in the 'A' Level Electronic Systems Course developed at Essex University. In 1976, after two years of trials in ten schools and colleges, Schools Council recognised Electronic Systems as a full 'A' Level subject quite distinct from any other 'A' Level discipline. This was the first full "systems" approach GCE course. Particularly due to the encouragement of industrial employers and certain local Education Authorities many schools and colleges have started to teach the course and over two hundred schools and colleges are now involved.

The concept of a "system" is fundamental to man and his world. The principles of systems analysis and modelling are applied in many fields of human endeavour including engineering (all branches), biology, ecology, meterology, sociology, human systems, medicine. The "systems" diagram of figure I defines the concept and some of the terms used to express it.

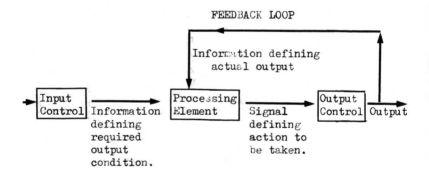

FEEDBACK LOOP

**Figure I: Electronic Systems Analysis**

Any "controlled" system is one which has an output which may be changed as a result of a demand from the input channelled through a processing element which also takes account of the current state of the output of the system. The examples included in the exponential technology chart all lend themselves to a systems approach understanding.

The operation of using information about the output state of the system is termed feedback. Feedback is essential for the control of any system. The feedback information together with the *command signal* is processed by the *decision-making element* or *brain* of the system. Information is conveyed between part of the system by means of communication links.

Scrutiny of the general system diagram reveals that there are three main areas of study in a systems course which are: *processing, feedback, communication.*

*Syllabus:*

*Processing Systems:* In this section emphasis is placed on decision making and the storage and retrieval of information. Computer and human problem solving processes are compared and particular strengths and weaknesses brought out. The structure and operation of digital systems are described with discussion ranging from large systems to dedicated microprocessor applications.

*Feedback Systems:* This section is concerned with the effects of using a signal defining the existing output of a system in the control of the systems response. Reference is made to positive feedback but the main emphasis is on negative feedback as a means of producing a desired stable situation. The human body is a prolific source of practical examples of feedback systems and furthermore, the human being as an entity, is often the central component in an overall feedback system, e.g., when driving a vehicle or controlling a machine.

The processes are explained and quantified in terms of electronic feedback in amplifiers and electromechanical servomechanisms.

*Communication Systems:* This section is concerned with the inherent need for communication between the elements of a system. The main characteristics of the basic human facilities of speech, hearing and vision are discussed and it is shown that both visual and audio information communication require a carrier to propagate energy, which is then modulated by the information to be communicated. This concept of modulation of a carrier is shown to be fundamental to all methods of transmitting information and is illustrated in detail in terms of the principles of television and sound broadcasting.

In subject material terms this 'A' Level course is intended to convey an appreciation and understanding of the impact of electronic systems on our way of life and to show that the general concepts and principles of systems analysis are applicable to man-made and natural systems, including man himself. The considerable breadth and relevance of the syllabus material makes the course interesting and of fundamental education significance. In intellectual terms, the course aims to develop the logical thinking capabilities of the student particularly the ability to relate ideas and concepts to design problems as well as in analysis. In terms of subject content and

**163**

approach 'A' Level Electronic Systems constitutes an advanced "Technology Awareness" course.

Electronic Systems may be taken in combination with Science subjects as a basis for further studies in Science and Engineering. It may also be studied with arts subjects as a broad educational discipline for those who intend to adopt careers in commerce, banking, management etc.

It is a feature of the 'A' Level Electronic Systems that the fundamental systems principles are demonstrated through extensive practical work. With each section of the course is a specially designed programme of experiments comprising fourteen five hour experiments. Each student also spends a total of 20 hours on one or two individual investigations/projects of his own choosing. The highly motivating content and practical nature of this course make it distinctly well suited to these aims.

## CEE Electronics - a top down systems approach

The five Southern GCE Boards, working jointly, have produced a series of CEE courses which includes an Electronics syllabus. The Southern Universities Joint Board is responsible for examining this. The development group responsible for the syllabus decided from the outset that this highly practically based course should start each section of work with a full working system which demonstrated to the pupils the overall concept of the particular study. They then proceed to examine the elements of the system and their integral operation either at a component level or at a systems level dependent on the system's complexity.

The four syllabus sections are:

### Section 1  The Radio Receiver and its Components

In this section the pupils examine a complete radio receiver and then study separately through practical investigation, selection, demodulation, amplification and then the derivation from the AC source of low voltage power to drive the radio system.

### Section 2  Oscillation

The concept of feedback is demonstrated using acoustic feedback in a system of a coupled microphone and loudspeaker amplifier system. This leads to a study of a tuned circuit oscillator and relaxation oscillators. The astable multivibrator is used to introduce the transistor in operation as an electronic switch.

### Section 3  Integrated Circuits

The operational amplifier is introduced as a device which can conveniently do many of the tasks for which transistors have been used. Their use in a system operating as an amplifier, comparator, oscillator driver and adder in particular is studied.

**164**

Digital integrated circuits are introduced through a traffic light system which embodies all the major elements of a digital system; namely a control sequence (program) derived from a shift register or binary counter decoded by a combinational logic system.

The examination consists of two written examinations, a practical examination aimed at establishing the level of pupils' skills in interpreting a practical electronic task defined on paper and implementing it and finally a practical project. The course introduces the system concept and many functional elements to the pupils who are then able for an examined project, to design and create a system to meet their own concept and specification.

As with many syllabuses in technology the Examination Boards have felt it useful and necessary to provide "notes for guidance" to help a teacher interpret the syllabus and to adopt an appropriate teaching approach.

## AEB 'O' Level Electronics

The AEB 'O' Level Electronics syllabus was examined for the first time in June 1982. The first entry was remarkable for a new subject: 2500 provisional which firmed up to 1900 actual candidates. This figure appears to be doubled for the 1983 entry. This syllabus uses a systems approach deliberately avoiding the analytic applied physics approach of many electricity and electronics syllabuses. The syllabus requires the student to develop an understanding of and use modern integrated circuits. The project work of the student can then result in the production of significant, interesting sophisticated electronic systems which could include micro-processor based systems. This further enhances the sense of relevance and motivating excitement and enjoyment embodied in student centred design project work, a feature of all of the new technology syllabuses.

It is significant that this syllabus and associated teacher support materials were developed with the active involvement and sponsorship of the Institution of Electrical Engineers (I.E.E.). When the syllabus was published it was introduced through teachers' conferences sponsored by the I.E.E., D.o.I. (Department of Industry) and E.I.T.B. (Engineering Industry Training Board).

The detailed syllabus is listed under the headings of Safety, Electrical Circuit Theory, Electronic Components, Practical Concepts, Building blocks for Electronic Systems, Synthesis of Building Blocks, Electronics in Society. The syllabus brings out the concepts of Information Technology and highlights the relationship between the digital systems of 'New Technology' and the analogue human world. The Electronics in Society section begins with a compulsory section on information representation and provides a choice from three options to enable a detailed study of one. These options are: The Telephone System, Radio Communication and Computer Systems.

**165**

## Other Electronics Syllabuses

Virtually every examination board now offers syllabuses in electronics or electricity and electronics at 'O', 'AO' levels or both. The Cambridge Board are introducing an 'A' level Electronics syllabus for examination for the first time in 1984. The 'AO' syllabus developments are significant in that many science sixth forms are studying an electronics course at this level to complement their specialist study of science.

Until recently most science courses did not incorporate any technological element in generally intensively over-academic syllabuses. The new compulsory core syllabus concept for physics means that some study of electronics will feature as part of the traditional pure science study. Hopefully teachers will utilise this opportunity to introduce this study with a truly technological flavour. The Cambridge Board has certainly taken this new innovation very seriously and besides incorporating a significantly wide ranging content to the electronics core module have also provided the necessary training courses to enable the teachers to get to grips with this new element required of their teaching skills.

The contrasting working procedures of the AEB and the Oxford Local Examination Board are interesting. The AEB 'O' level syllabus was developed by a committee of schoolteachers, lecturers from higher education, engineers and industrial representatives. The syllabus was, therefore conceived, devised, refined by consultation and then "put into the syllabus book" as a full mode I. The Oxford Board at the same period of time as this syllabus was being written allowed individual schools to produce mode III syllabuses. As a result of the collective experience of a number of entrepreneurial teachers of actually teaching the subject, mode I syllabuses were finally devised. The Oxford Board have both an 'O' and 'AO' syllabus. The 'AO' being largely devised as a suitable first year sixth form course leading into the 'A' level electronic systems course. The 'A' level work can then be completed as a one year follow-on study. It also gives the students the opportunity to discontinue their study of electronics after one year in the sixth form whilst still having the opportunity to gain a qualification for the work already completed. In some sixth forms after a one year study of this 'AO' syllabus they choose to study either 'A' level Electronic Systems or Computer Studies in their second year.

## AEB 'A' Level Endorsement

This syllabus is intended for those students wishing to follow a course in electronics as an addition to their advanced level study and has been in existence for a considerable time.

The examination may be taken as an endorsement to any one of the following advanced level subjects: Physics, Physical Science, Engineering Science, Electronic Systems or Computer Science. The examination consists of one three hour paper, and in order to qualify for a pass candidates must be successful in one of the above subjects together with the endorsement paper.

The endorsement is considered to be equivalent to approximately half an 'A' level and the bias of the current syllabus is deliberately towards the physics of semiconductor devices. Major topics include the band theory of solids, the structure of semiconductor material and semiconductor devices and the fabrication of integrated circuits.

Transistors are considered in some detail, together with operational amplifiers, feedback oscillators, rectifiers and electron optics.

There is a small section on digital processing which includes a study of the logic gate, half adder and binary counting. The present syllabus is under review and it is likely that the revised syllabus which will be examined for the first time in 1987, will have much greater emphasis on digital electronics, covering in detail topics such as combinational and sequential logic, microprocessors and microprocessor systems.

**"Microelectronics For All"**

As first conceived the ECT domain of M.E.P. was largely concerned with curriculum development and in-service teacher training for the new courses appearing in the curriculum labelled Electronics, Control Technology and Electronic Systems. At that time electronics/microelectronics was increasingly appearing in the syllabus of physics, engineering ecience, craft design and technology. The major limiting factor to the adequate teaching of these subjects had been the lack of curriculum materials and lack of teacher expertise. The domain activity is now increasingly being occupied with support for the development of courses to be included in the 11-14 curriculum for all pupils aimed at technology awareness and variously titled "Microelectronics for All", "Getting started in Electronics", "Starting Microelectronics".

The study of microelectronics as exemplified by most microelectronics for all courses does not require a preliminary study of the physics of electricity. However the inclusion of electronics in examination syllabuses, most notably the Nuffield 'A' level physics Unit 6 has stimulated an awareness amongst teachers of the implications of microelectronics for the whole curriculum. With it has developed an enthusiasm to learn and teach about microelectronics amongst very many teachers including some who might have previously regarded themselves as traditional. As a result there is a very rapidly growing, largely self developed, expertise in microelectronics evident amongst teachers. No other subject has, or possibly could, stimulate this degree of commitment to self education. This had led to what will possibly be the most significant impact of microelectronics on the curriculum, namely the inclusion of "Microelectronics for All" course in the curriculum of every secondary pupil. Those teachers who have taught children about

**167**

microelectronics, who have run electronics hobby clubs, who understand about the implications of microelectronics on the lives of everyone are quite convinced that MFA is as fundamental as the 3Rs to the "education for life" concept.

Given that the ideal of this concept is realised, as is already happening in some schools, an average secondary school will require at least twelve teachers with the necessary knowledge and expertise to make this provision for all pupils in the school.

*What is the nature of current "Microelectronics for All" courses*

The purpose of the MFA courses is to convey to pupils of all abilities an awareness of new technology, which might be defined as follows:

"An appreciation of the fundamental principles of new technology, how the application of the technology relates to human needs and complements human abilities and how the continued development and application of the technology will influence future patterns of living.

In this context the word 'technology', which literally means 'ways of doing things', refers to 'Information Technology' or 'Microelectronics Technology'."

The question then arises - what are these fundamental principles and how can they be presented to the pupils interestingly and effectively? Many schools' technology awareness courses are now being developed across the country. They are all based on or include a practical study of electronics incorporating a black box approach. The similarities of objectives and approaches are striking, bearing in mind that these developments only began conception two or three years ago in a largely uncoordinated manner. All take account of and capitalise on a number of common factors which include:

1.   The course must be acceptable, stimulating and meaningful to pupils of all abilities. Microelectronics investigated practically is singularly unique as a subject in making this possible.

2.   The course must give students the opportunity to construct electronic systems which they can understand, describe and modify. At one level this can be done with "modules" (ready assembled system blocks which simply require connection into a system) or at a higher level can involve system assembly utilising "naked" chips which are themselves functional system elements.

3.   The course must provide an understanding of binary information systems, the principles of logic operations, memory and programmable systems which is the key to the ability to interpret and appreciate new technology.

4. The course must provide an introduction to the subject and a foundation for those pupils who will choose to study microelectronics beyond the awareness level.

5. The course must include materials which deal with the social and economic consequences of the new technology, in particular the benefits of its application in industry.

The essence of the study is the simplicity of the basic ideas involved. Sophisticated electronic devices being treated as black boxes which have particular functions. It is of course axiomatic that an awareness of new technology must involve an appreciation of the difference in nature and capability of digital systems and the analogue nature of the ultimate information system, man himself. It is by man's efforts to meet man's needs that microelectronics technology has developed and evolved.

*Particular approaches in MFA*

It is a doubtful practice to isolate particular initiatives in this field for special mention since so many excellent schemes exist, all achieving the same objectives but with different approaches. Notes on the three schemes serve to describe the implementation of the general themes described above.

*Perryfields High Schools:* Four years ago basic electronics was introduced into the third year physics course. Interest and enthusiasm resulted in this being extended to microelectronics in the 2nd year course. The immediate problem was what equipment to use. Commercial items were expensive for class sets on schools' budgets and flexible systems tended to be complicated to use. As a result the course originator, David Thompson, designed his own hardware and pupil materials from scratch. This course emphasises the way in which electronics is applied in industry. This is achieved with support from local industry which supplies demonstration lectures at the school and covers a range of firms and topics. The spur for the development of this course came as a result of the D.o.I.'s 'Micros in Secondary Schools Scheme', which implied a need for a computer awareness course for all pupils but which does not provide the material means to achieve this.

*Rowlinson School, Sheffield:* The new extensive experience at Rowlinson School began with the idea that computing and the control application of computers deserved a place in the curriculum of every pupil. Work began with an experimental course taking eight periods from each of the second year mathematics and physics time. The micro chosen for this course at that time was the Open University PT501 (designed for introducing businessmen to the essentials of computing). Following an introduction to the essentials of the subject, i.e. binary codes, memory, address, register, accumulator,

**169**

programs, the pupils followed a sequence of problem solving exercises. From this work course modules have now been developed which appear at virtually every level of the curriculum from the first year upwards. As well as microelectronics and microcomputer control applications there are course modules on computer awareness, communication and information studies, microelectronics. This school has shown what can be achieved in a short time with a dedicated effort. I have frequently heard the school's headmaster say at conferences and debates - "You cannot say 'We don't have time', 'We don't have the expertise', 'We don't have the money'; Simply 'We must do something about educating pupils for the world of now and 2000'".

*Belper High School:* The "3-Chip" controller concept.

One of M.E.P.'s first supported curriculum development schemes was initiated at Belper High School by Peter Nicholls (now M.E.P. ECT INSET Co-ordinator, East Midlands). Here it was required to provide a course in microelectronics for an all ability CSE class which took account of the following facts:

1.  For every microprocessor built into a computer there are at least ten used in dedicated control systems based around a processor, a program memory, and an input-output unit.

2.  To enable a class of 20 pupils to experiment with micro-computer control requires 10 microcomputer systems costing perhaps £500 each. Much of the facility of the computer is unused by the pupil, and the wrong message is at the same time conveyed to him - that you need keyboards, VDUs, high level language and expensive hardware to control simple systems.

Because of these facts, Peter Nicholls developed a minimal microprocessor control system.

A range of plug-on units has also been designed which enable pupils to control a tone generator, a model railway, a 4 character display, motors (e.g. Lego or Meccano) and lamps (via a high power digital-analogue converter). An analogue-digital converter enables the construction of, for example, a digital thermometer. The equipment has been extensively trialled with all ability CSE classes during the school year '80-'81. This approach to control is suitable for any level of study, any age or ability of pupil.

## Microelectronics in Primary Schools

Readers will know of the "Micros in Primary" scheme. Many will also know of the use to which the programmable toy "Big Track" is being put to develop spatial awareness, ideas of geometry, numeracy, the concept of planning a course of events. The story does not end there. BBC Radiovision are working on a Primary School Microelectronics course. Notes will be available in July 1983 and the course could start in September 1983. There are primary schools already beginning to introduce some aspects of practical Electronics in their normal curriculum. Graham Bickerton, Headmaster of Alsager County Primary School, has developed his own practical course for a microelectronics option for some pupils. This is now well tried and very popular. He does not run a watered down degree course, the objectives and approach are not the same as in the secondary school. The involvement and achievement of the pupils, even those of the most limited ability, provides self evident justification that this is a powerful and suitable medium for primary pupils.

### Courses with "Technology" in Their Title

Many different courses at CSE, 'O' and 'A' level are now being taught including Control Technology, Modular Technology, Craft Design and Technology, Technology. These courses are frequently taught in the schools' technology departments which in years gone by were responsible for courses in woodwork, metalwork, technical drawing. These courses embrace the concept of technology as being ways of doing things in a much wider sense than microelectronics technology. Students variously study mechanisms, structures, gears, pneumatics, aeronautics, electronics and more recently microelectronics. The microelectronic study in these courses is tending to have a particular identity and flavour which is different from the electronics/microelectronics approach of syllabus titled such and is more associated with the concept of control technology. The microelectronic control technology concept is about the use of digital electronic systems to produce signals which operate devices external to the electronic processing block. In this context, for some, the electronic processing block is simply a computer with VDU and keyboard. Such a study forms a useful basis to an appreciation of the nature of programmable control systems. However it belies the inherent simplicity of the control concept and the fact that the majority of micros are not used in the manufacture of personal computers but form part of dedicated electronic systems. The whole basis of the silicon chip revolution is that a sophisticated, cheap, small electronic processing block may be simply constrained to perform particular defined tasks. Examples are in the washing machine and virtually every electronic system now manufactured. There are very many microprocessors controlling modern video-recorders.

Control Technology and Modular Technology are the titles of GCE 'O' level subjects. Examined by a number of GCE Boards with various approaches, uptake of these courses is increasing rapidly. The overall entry for the 1983 examinations will probably be of the order of 6000 candidates.

### Microelectronics "Modular Technology" Course

The "Modular Technology" syllabuses have a core syllabus of

**171**

compulsory basic topics which are - energy, materials and problem solving and each school chooses options from a range of equivalent courses which are studied in detail. One advantage of this system is that new modules may be produced to incorporate new ideas or changes in technology. Since the modules are optional this gives time for teachers new to the subject to develop their expertise before introducing the subject into their teaching. The Schools Council Modular Technology Project began in 1970 and the work on a "Microelectronics Module" began in 1979. The module was required to reflect the increasing application of microelectronics and computer control in industry. The development team, led by Tim Pike of the Ramsden Boys School, was faced with a number of limiting parameters. These were:

1.   The module should be able to be taught in twelve weeks.

2.   The unit cost of hardware should be as low as possible and certainly cheap enough for class sets to be practicable.

3.   No prior knowledge should be assumed of either the pupil or the teacher.

No suitable hardware was available at the time and a specific design was developed (by a commercial concern) to meet the module requirements. The system, called the "MENTA", incorporated the following significant features; the programming can be done in either machine code or assembler rather than BASIC, the device is based on the X80 chip and uses a normal TV for display.
    The MENTA is used with peripheral systems to simulate industrial control systems. This work frequently forms the subject of a project problem which is part of the course examination. The course itself aims to teach about number systems, logic functions, microcomputer architecture, control principles, digital and analogue processes and interfacing techniques.
    An optional module based on this approach is now available with a number of examined modular technology courses both at GCE and CSE level.
    This development was one of the first M.E.P. supported hardware/examination syllabus developments.

**Structured Courses in "Control Technology"**

Control Technology is a subject which has similar objectives to modular technology but has a fixed compulsory syllabus.
    The teaching approach of the structured course is one of progressive problem solving. The pupils are guided through a series of basic blocks of knowledge and experience, by working through assignments and project work. They are supplied with work assignment sheets, which are not a simple recipe of instructions, but statements and questions which break down each problem into stages

which pupils should be able to solve. Written records of their results and conclusions are made. On the completion of each assignment, "follow-up" sheets are issued, which explain the solutions they could have arrived at, suggests alternative solutions and give examples of the application of the knowledge gained.

The original syllabus includes a study of Structures, Motion and Mechanisms, Electricity, Pneumatic Control, Logic.

Technology Microprocessor Control is a new revision of this course designed to provide the knowledge and design experience associated with the control of mechanical, electrical, electronic and microprocessor devices.

Many of our domestic appliances such as fridges, washing machines, food mixers etc., contain electrical microprocessor control systems. The industrial application of computer control systems is becoming extensive. This course is directed towards this aspect of technology. The new course includes Structures, Mechanisms, and Electricity in a similar way to the original syllabus but then goes on to study Logic, Programming, Interfacing and Social Implications. This latter section is a significant addition to the philosophy of the course and is an essential element to any technology syllabus which purports to be "educational".

Both of these courses require the pupil to complete a major project as part of the examination procedure. M.E.P. has supported the development of this course both at NCST (the National Centre for Schools Technology) and at Doncaster where the first Control Technology course originated.

### Where is "Microelectronics in Schools" Heading?

Quite clearly the developments in electronics teaching are wide ranging and diverse. Since this is a new subject to all levels of teaching and since the principles being taught are intrinsically simple and available to a wide range of ability and age there is, at present, no coherent progressive knowledge structure throughout the education system. The work currently being done at Alsager County Primary School gives a knowledge and understanding which would be a welcome addition to education of the many secondary pupils for whom microelectronics is at present "Tomorrows World" and Christmas present kit experience or perhaps even less than that. Work being done in some higher education courses as part of science or engineering study in some cases is on a par to that being competently taught and learnt in technology courses in schools. This is particularly true in the areas of microprocessor control and robotics.

It is known to have been said to students being interviewed when applying for higher education places, "you should stick to academic subjects and leave the technology to us". A desperate cry from an admissions tutor perhaps worried about the ability of the Institution to cope with pupils already well advanced into the subject of microelectronics. It is not just software writing that able sixth formers seem to be able to master as well or better than adults. Of course the "leave it to us" argument is nonsense and denies the importance of a wide ranging experience of information technology and its implication for the education of all. If this view was accepted what proportion of the population would know about new technology? How would the technologists and engineers required to service an industrial economy come to establish their careers whilst still at school?

The lack of a clear structuring of levels of education in microelectronics is due to a number of factors, most notably a very variable teacher experience and competence in the subject. It is remarkable how quickly enthusiastic teachers become very knowledgeable and advanced in this art when once the subject has been opened to them. This widens the gap between those that know and those that don't know.

Another factor is the very variable levels of evolvement and consequent demand of subjects entitled Electronics, Microelectronics, Technology, appearing in the curriculum. The approach and level sometimes reflects the course developers' lack of confidence and experience and in other cases the enthusiastic enterprise of the rapidly advancing new "technologist teacher". The half life of a technology syllabus in the current state of flux is probably only 5-10 years. There is also a particular danger in that there are pupils who progress exceptionally rapidly; they must not be permitted to establish standards beyond the reach of the majority. Because some pupils can does not mean all pupils should. We must not end up with syllabuses so overfull and advanced as is the case for much of the academic curriculum that the extent of knowledge is the key to success and not the degree of understanding.

One thing which is very certain is that the rapid development and uptake of new courses will continue. Teachers are finding that practical microelectronics is singularly well fitted to motivate and stimulate pupils in a quite unprecedented way and that this extends across the ability and age range. It exemplifies the statement frequently quoted but infrequently incorporated into an overacademic education system.

"Tell me and I will forget; teach me and I will remember; show me and let me try it for myself and I will understand".

## APPENDIX ONE

### The Microcomputer System

*CPU*
A computer system consists of input and output devices, a central processing unit or **CPU** and a memory. This collection of devices is referred to as the computer **hardware.** Instructions are communicated to the machine in the form of a computer **program** (software) which can be written in a variety of computer languages each with its own rules of grammar and syntax.

There are various types of computer memory. *RAM* Every computer has a **RANDOM ACCESS MEMORY** or **RAM** of a particular size. The important characteristic of this memory is that information can be transferred to or obtained directly from any given place (address) in the RAM without having to pass other addresses. A computer's RAM is incorporated on silicon chips inside the machine. Random access memory is not permanent - it is volatile in that all information stored in it is lost once the computer is switched off. Computers *ROM* also contain internal **READ ONLY MEMORY** or **ROM.** The ROM contains special information that is available for reading only and which cannot under normal circumstances be changed or supplemented. The ROM usually contains information that is used very frequently. For example, many computers store the BASIC language in a ROM. Read-only memory is of course non-volatile. A computer's total internal 'working' memory (RAM and ROM) is strictly limited in size.

When a number or a letter for example is entered into the computer, it is coded automatically into a series of 0's and 1's - i.e. a series of binary digits or **bits** as they are called. For most computers 8 binary digits are used to uniquely specify a particular piece of information. There are 256 possible combinations of eight 0's and 1's from 00000000 to 11111111. The *ASCII CODE* American Standard Code for Information Interchange or **ASCII** code uses 128 of these combinations. For

**175**

example, the letter A is coded as 01000001 and a question mark as 00111111. The 8 digit code for a piece of information is called a **BYTE**. Most microcomputers have a maximum internal memory of 64,000 (64K) bytes which is usually adequate as a working memory but too small for storing a library of programs or files of data. Consequently each computer has peripheral (external) memory storage, which can be accessed via the keyboard.

*BYTE*

There are two main types of peripheral storage devices currently in use with microcomputers. A magnetic **tape** device stores information on ordinary audio cassette tape. Information from the computer's internal memory can be stored on the magnetic tape, whilst pre-recorded information can be loaded from tape into the computer's internal memory. This method is cheap but often unreliable and relatively slow. Also there is no *direct* access to a program stored on the tape. Magnetic **disk** storage records information on a circular magnetic disk. A disk **drive** rotates the disk rapidly and information is recorded or read from the disk by a head that can be positioned anywhere along the radius of the disk. Most microcomputers use small flexible 'floppy' disks which are reliable and cheap to buy. Access to a program recorded on a disk is direct and rapid. Typically disks hold about 100,000 (100K) bytes of information.

*TAPE*

*DISK*
*DRIVE*

To communicate with a computer one has to use one of the many computer languages available and one that a particular microcomputer can understand. Microcomputers can accept only a limited number of languages of which **BASIC** (Beginners All-Purpose Sequential Interaction Code) is the most common.

*BASIC*

Programming languages are usually devised for a particular application. **FORTRAN** is usually used in science and engineering, **COBOL** in business and data processing. BASIC was designed for the novice programmer, whilst **PASCAL** is a well structured language that is often used to write educational programs. **LOGO** and **PILOT** are more 'user-friendly' languages that are easy to learn yet very powerful programming tools. While BASIC is common to all microcomputers only recently have other languages become available on small machines. For languages other than BASIC larger internal memories are needed; such language capabilities are becoming increasingly available on today's microcomputers but at additional expense. In most cases this additional cost represents only a small fraction of the initial outlay.

Not only are computers useful for manipulating

*STRING* numbers, but they are extremely valuable in manipulating text, that is, sentences, words and characters. A sequence of characters is called a **STRING**. Strings can be stored in the memory of the computer and manipulated in much the same way as numbers.

*FILE* When large amounts of data are to be manipulated, it is customary to use a **FILE**. Much like an ordinary file, a computer file is an area in the computer's memory allocated for the storage and retrieval of information. The information stored in a file may be data or a computer program.

# APPENDIX TWO

## Glossary

| | |
|---|---|
| **Address** | The name of a storage location in the computer memory. |
| **Algorithm** | A sequence of instructions for solving a problem. |
| **Bubble Memory** | A device for storing large amounts of data. The information is retained when the computer is switched off. |
| **Buffer** | A temporary storage area between a peripheral device and the central processor. |
| **Bug** | An error. A software bug is an error in logic or syntax in a computer program. A hardware bug is a fault in the equipment. |
| **Chip** | A complex electronic circuit built on a thin slice of silicon. |
| **Cursor** | A small flashing rectangle or line on the computer video terminal that indicates the current display position. |
| **Daisy Wheel Printer** | A printer that produces high quality type. The characters are mounted on the perimeter of a wheel. |
| **Debugging** | The process of finding and correcting bugs. |
| **DOS** | Disk Operating System. A program which controls the interaction of the computer with its disk drive. |

**Dot Matrix Printer**
A printer that forms characters as a pattern of individual dots rather than solid lines.

**EPROM**
Erasable Programmable **ROM.** A read-only memory that can be erased.

**Execute**
To carry out the instructions specified by a program.

**Graphics**
The pictorial representation of information.

**Graphics Tablet**
An input device which allows the user to input directly drawings or characters into the computer.

**High-Level Language**
A programming language that uses commands which approximate to the English language (e.g. BASIC, FORTRAN).

**Ink Jet Printer**
A rapid high quality printer in which a stream of electrically charged ink droplets are deflected by a magnetic field.

**Intelligent Terminal**
A terminal that can process data to a limited extent independently of the mainframe computer to which it is linked.

**Interface**
The hardware or software that enables a computer to communicate to a peripheral device.

**Line Printer**
A printer that prints an entire line of type simultaneously, rather than a single character.

**Load**
To transfer information from one part of a computer system to another, for example, from a peripheral storage device to the computer memory.

**Low-Level Language**
A programming language close to the instructions recognised directly by the computer.

**Mainframe Computer**
A large and very powerful computer.

| | |
|---|---|
| **Menu** | A list of programs stored on a tape or disk. |
| **Monitor** | A video display unit. |
| **Network** | The sharing of resources (e.g. disk drive) by two or more computers. |
| **Peripheral Device** | A device such as a printer or disk drive which communicates with the central processing unit. |
| **Port** | A connection which allows input and output lines to be attached to the computer. |
| **PROM** | Programmable **ROM**. |
| **RUN** | The command which instructs a computer to commence the execution of a program. |
| **Scrolling** | The movement of text up or down the screen for viewing. |
| **Syntax** | The grammatical rules associated with a programming language. |
| **Terminal** | A device used for communicating with a computer. |
| **Turn Key** | A computer system that is in an operational mode immediately it is switched on. |
| **Word Processing** | The process of entering, editing and storing text. |
| **Workspace** | An area for the temporary storage of data for immediate use. |